STORIES OF SPIRITUAL HEALING

Becoming Well

KWANG-HEE PARK

With continuous content feedback by Norma Fain Pratt and Jochen Strack

SacraSage Press (SacraSagePress.com)

Cover Photo: Hume Lake, CA, by Karsten van Sander (with Mitchel Cox)
Interior Design: Nicole Sturk
Cover Design: ProDesigns

Print (Paperback): 978-1-948609-46-3
Electronic: 978-1-948609-65-4

Printed in the United States of America

Library of Congress Cataloguing-in-Publication Data

STORIES OF SPIRITUAL HEALING: BECOMING WELL / KWANG-HEE PARK

A heartfelt Thank You to:

Norma Fain Pratt and my husband Jochen Strack for their continuous content feedback; to copywriter Maddie Gavel-Briggs; and to Evelyn McClave, Karsten van Sander, Jong-shin Park, Hanna Strack, Hans-Dieter Strack, Dirk Kloss, Joe Bautista, and Gisela Nuernberg for their proofreading and great questions.

All stories are based on real-life anecdotes. Names of persons have been changed and some stories are autobiographical. Printed with permission of the main protagonists. We are very grateful to them and hope that others will find healing through their stories!

Content

Introduction 1

(1) Then Forgiving Comes by Itself 7

(2) I Grow My Backbone 11

(3) How Marlin Discovered Herself in Brian and
Reoriented Her Life 15

(4) I Give Space. Thus, I Receive Space 19

(5) Julia's Inner Voice Leads Her Further 23

(6) A Letter That is Bringing Joy 29

(7) What Elaine Was Really Searching for 35

(8) A Spiritual Companionship 39

(9) The Night Jesus Visited 45

(10) Jinny's Inner Voice Gives Her Heart Peace 49

(11) A Holy Mark 53

(12) Reunion. 57

(13) Sometimes the Real Gift Comes from Someone
You Never Even Thought of. 63

(14) How a Fairly Inappropriate Laugh Led to a
Feeling of Acceptance 67

(15) Sophia Finds Communion with the Holy Spirit
and People 71

(16) A Hurdle Becomes a Blessing 75

(17) Doris' Role as Mother Changed 79

(18) Tania Finds Her Calling and Reveals God as the
Nurturer 83

(19) A Compassionate Presence. 87

(20) What Really Matters 93

(21) Dietrich Experiences His Passion in a New Way . . . 99

(22) Martin Realizes What Carries Him 105

(23) A Humble Blessing 109

(24) How Can I Find Something That is Very Dear to
Me Again?. 113

(25) The Inherent Dignity of Everyone. 117

(26) Abundant Life. 121

(27) How Martha's Sadness Over Not Conceiving
Her Own Child Led Her to Herself 125

(28) Marlon Restores Her Strength 129

(29) Caroline Discerns How to Prioritize Her Work. . . . 133

(30) In Great Despair 137

(31) Sue and Robert Give and Receive 143

(32) Salome Reopens Her Heart 149

(33) Awakening 153

(34) A Five-Minute Prayer 159

(35) Jeremy Finds the Love He Sought for So Long. . . . 165

(36) An Amazing Team Spirit. 169

(37) Emma Thinks About Everything Again 175

(38) The Dash Is What Matters. 181

(39) Grace Experiences How She Can Appreciate
That of Others and Her Own. 185

(40) The Common Plot 189

(41) Healing 193

Appendix: On Prayer and Discernment 199

Introduction

Healing is the process of recovering from wounds. A person experiences healing in many different ways. Wounds can have many causes, such as a dysfunctional family, trauma, a beloved one's unexpected passing, abuse, or abandonment during childhood, divorce, or loss of parents. Setbacks in career and employment can also cause wounds.

Wounds can lead to depression, lack of self-esteem, and attitudes that hinder growth, both for the individual and for those around them. Wounds often remain buried and express themselves in harmful behavior to oneself or others. Ultimately, they may cause an empty soul.

Whether wounds have been inflicted by external or internal processes, they will affect the person's physical and emotional well-being, and may lead to spiritual confusion and the questioning of the presence of God. Such an impact of wounds upon a person's mind, body, and spirit may be conscious, subconscious, or even unconscious.

Conversely, healing is experiencing the energy of life again. For some, healing happens quickly—such as in a shallow cut of the skin that will heal in a couple of days.

The healing of a wounded soul, however, can be a lifelong process.

Healing has been an important theme in my own life. I have experienced different wounds: My parents' separation, my broken relationships, and a desire to be loved and respected in society as a woman. At times I felt helpless; I longed to restore my life energy.

It was a difficult process as I struggled to get out of dark valleys, hoping to see light again. Even though I spent years studying pastoral counseling, academic training itself was not enough to heal my wounds. Emigrating from Korea to the United States brought its own challenges culturally, emotionally, financially, and spiritually.

A personal encounter with Jesus and daily prayer practice slowly untangled my issues one by one. Prayer led me on a spiritual path to experience healing and to find who I am in God. Through this process, I found my calling as a healer.

As a chaplain, counselor, adjunct professor, and Oriental medicine health care provider I have been privileged to listen to the stories of women and men from various cultural and ethnic backgrounds. Some stories were painful; others were energizing and delightful. Listening to these personal stories was a powerful channel that brought insights towards healing and reconciliation. Each person's story showed how healing took place in their unique way.

In this book, I have portrayed some of the stories I have been entrusted with as well as some of my own. All names have been changed.

For some people, relief of emotional stress brings physical restoration as well. One of the stories in this book shows how that person's physical pain was in fact a disguised cry to resolve their unspoken emotional pain. For others, feeling empty or depressed is a yearning for deeper meaning and values beyond their daily routines. It is a spiritual issue and often their beginning to seek and find God as the source of meaning and life.

As a person begins to share their story, the process of sharing enables him or her to enter into their inner world with courage. Hidden parts of one's life begin to come forward. It is not always easy to find a thread that will mend a broken and painful life, but the many pieces of the puzzle of life will gradually form a coherent picture.

While I listened to these diverse life experiences, I saw glimpses of the Divine presence. Those who were in darkness struggled to find renewed balance in their lives. Listening is itself a form of care.

Spiritual direction is a particular kind of attentive listening where one person provides a safe haven for another person to talk about their true self. The listener's genuine interest, love, and acceptance allow the sharer to experience a transforming power that nurtures their self and others. Their image of God may become one of love, instead of fear. Through the care of the listener, God draws us to choosing hope over despair.

The person listening and the person sharing are connected through a caring heart. Healing becomes a joint process between the storyteller and the listener. It is the process of awakening and cultivating insights and Divine wisdom deep within each of us. It is the process of restoring the power of life in each of us.

In due time, healing will not be confined to oneself. It will open spiritual eyes, seeing the pain of others and standing by the broken-hearted. Thus, a compassionate heart emerges out of the healing process and empowers others.

When I listened to the energy of life returning to a person, there always seemed to be healing not only for the individual but also for their family, friends, and even for God. A compassionate heart is a Divine gift.

Such compassion can be strengthened with a spiritual practice, for example, prayer. For some, prayer may be heavily tainted from prior negative and oppressive religious experiences. A simple way of praying, however, such as silently repeating the word "Love" or "Peace of God," can turn prayer into a joyful experience that brings energy and peace in times of trial.

As prayer becomes a daily practice, it includes both talking as well as listening to God, a kind of spiritual conversation with God. It takes time and practice until prayer becomes the opening of a new day.

Many stories in this book tell of persons who entered into a life of prayer and thereby experienced self-transforming power. Praying naturally invites us to start an inner journey that enables us to confront pain and inner wounds. Likewise, praying will also foster the rediscovery of strengths and resources. Divine light and wisdom will shine upon us.

Praying with others in a group is also a way towards healing. Members of a group talk about their issues and concerns, pray for one another, cry and laugh together, and thus share their burdens with each other and with God. Such a prayer group promotes reflection and mutual growth. An empowering spiritual community—whether big or small—lifts the spirit and rekindles the energy of life.

When we are aware of the presence of the Divine, our mundane daily lives become more meaningful and encouraging. I remember a painting on the wall of a friend's house. It shows an angel who with all her strength connects two broken bars. The friend said, "This painting reflects my brokenness and weakness. The angel is trying to hold the two broken parts of my life so that I may not fall." The painting reminded him of the Divine presence that holds and sustains him.

We feel we are not alone when we sense that the Divine is present, holding us, healing our brokenness, and strengthening our weakness.

After each story, I ask the reader to reflect on aspects of their own journey towards healing. You may receive insights that will generate a transformative power to bring forth new life. A short prayer at the end of each story suggests ways for finding wisdom within yourself and through Divine guidance. When you draw upon it, your body, mind, and spirit will feel at peace, connected with God, whole and holy.

(1)

Then Forgiving Comes by Itself

"In my heart of hearts, God is closer to me than I am to myself."

—Augustine (354–430)

Kay created a bi-weekly women's prayer group: Four or five women with diverse ethnic backgrounds gathered and shared their life concerns. They prayed for one another in silence or aloud.

Every time a different woman volunteered to be the facilitator for the evening; once it was a Jewish lady's turn to lead the prayer group. Louise and her older sister lost most of her Russian and Polish family and relatives during the Holocaust. She asked the group to take half an hour to write an autobiographical story about forgiveness in their lives.

Kay became immersed in thought over the word "Forgiveness." Strangely enough, no one person came to her mind. True, she had been hurt by broken relationships when former boyfriends left her because of a lack of commitment or other women. But she never felt the need to forgive them to cultivate her spiritual well-being. She also dismissed the reasons for these unsuccessful relationships as behavioral problems or cultural issues stemming from a failure of men and women to understand each other. When she thought about them, she would become depressed and sad.

Eventually, Kay developed her own method to heal her pain. She prayed alone or with others. She came up with a ritual to start her days with a prayer. Her prayer time became longer and longer, from five minutes to 30 minutes and then to one hour and sometimes even several hours. As time passed, she no longer focused on her depression or on the boyfriends whom she thought had caused her pain.

She felt guided by a profound spiritual sense. She thought it to be the Holy Spirit. In her meditation, the word "Hamartia" arose. The Greek root of the word means "to miss the mark," and is often used to define sin.

It was an awakening moment for her. She realized when she would "miss the mark," she became obsessively fixed on bitterness, regrets, unresolved sadness, fears, and despair which she thought was caused by the former boyfriends. Her prayer life helped her healing. She became in touch with spiritual feelings, especially with the love of God.

Kay was delighted to release her obsessions. Closing her eyes, she saw an image: A small, new heart growing within a broken heart. The little heart became bigger and the broken heart gradually peeled off. In the image, her daily prayer was the channel through which the love of

God flowed into her inner small heart. She would simply lay out all her concerns in front of God and then listen.

Deep peace, a small voice, images, and insights arose. They encouraged her, consoled her heart, guided her mind, and strengthened her. Now she understood why she didn't make or even force herself to forgive her former boyfriends. She didn't need to. Forgiving came to her.

She shared her insight with the group, "For me, forgiveness is not an active effort. Rather, it comes naturally to me when my heart is filled with the love of God."

Spiritual Practice

(1) Write a short autobiographical story on forgiveness. Allow 20 to 30 minutes to write your story. If you need more time, keep writing.

(2) Imagine you are reading your story to God. Write what you heard as a reply.

(3) What might be your channels into which Divine love can flow?

Prayer

God, here are all my hurts. Hold my wounded heart in Your love so that my broken heart will be filled with Your love and recover joy again.

(2)

I Grow My Backbone

"This is to me the hour of greatest joy I ever had in this world. No ear can hear, no tongue can utter, and no heart can understand the sweet incomes and the refreshing of the spirit of the Lord, which I now feel."

—Mary Dyer (1611–1660)

Thomas was attracted to theology after he experienced the profound sharing of personal recoveries in Alcoholics Anonymous groups. He also felt a satisfying sense of natural flow whenever he contributed his thoughts in conversations about God and faith.

But his personal problems and struggles with previous relationships made him feel insecure, often fragile, and vulnerable. He worked with a psychotherapist and was glad for that. One day he saw a course in chaplaincy offered at a hospital in Hawai'i and he imagined he would find some of the answers he sought there. Hawai'i, he thought, with the ocean waves, the rainbows in the mountains, and the volcanic land still growing, was a place where spirituality came naturally.

The chaplaincy program, however, was more demanding than he expected. By the end of the spring semester, he needed to rejuvenate his energies to feel peaceful. The outdoors was Thomas' place and he reveled in the quiet experience of nature: the ocean, trees, gentle rain, birds, and surfing all comforted him.

He invited his girlfriend Melanie to visit a friend's farm with him where they could camp together. She was delighted and accepted immediately. Thomas prepared for their camping adventure by gathering an air mattress, water bottles, flashlight, tablecloth, cooking utensils, and of course, coffee. When they arrived on the farm, their friend Jim welcomed them, and they spent some time visiting together.

Thomas wanted to set up the tent before it got dark. The site was not at ground level but was instead situated on an elevated wooden platform, surrounded by a side rail overlooking a valley. Thomas and Melanie had to climb up several steps. As they pitched their tent, they were surrounded by the wide-open nature. "What fresh air!" they exclaimed as Thomas took a deep breath.

They woke up early the next morning. The sun was out and they began to prepare breakfast. It was a beautiful place. Thomas was happy to be able to use his old camping pot, a gift from a friend. The sound of boiling water, the smell of coffee, and birds singing in the trees made the couple feel rested. Melanie said, "What a gorgeous and

peaceful place this is!" They started to eat a simple breakfast together.

Deep in conversation, Melanie pointed to the side rail
that surrounded the wooden platform of their camp. She
said, "Thomas, look at these two diagonal bars here that
hold up the top bar of the rail. I feel that you are like these
diagonal bars: a bit off-center and not grounded. But if you
practice prayer, then you will be like these other two verti-
cal bars here in the middle that hold up the top rail. A life
of prayer will give you a strong back, so to speak. You will
be centered in God." This thought reached deep down into
Thomas' core. He thought to himself, "With such a prayer
life, I may no longer need to depend on psychotherapy and
medication. I may still need to consult with my therapist,
but I think I will be able to develop my true core in God and
with God."

In time, Thomas developed a firm desire to ground his
life in prayer. He called it his backbone theory—centering
in God with a daily prayer.

He stayed and worked on the farm a while longer.
Every morning he took the time to sit quietly and pray,
"God, Your healing touch be with me today. Help me to be
centered in You."

One day a young boy named Tim came by on the way
to the summer program at the elementary school near the
farm. Thomas greeted Tim, "How are you doing today?"
The boy looked at him and was silent for a while and answered, "Good. I feel connected with God this morning."
Thomas was curious, "How do you know you are connected with God?" The boy pointed to his abdomen and

said, "Whenever I see my navel, I remember a dream that I had when I was in my mother's womb where I am connected with a long string to God in heaven." Thomas remembered what he realized on the campsite platform and was touched by what the boy said.

Two months later, Thomas was working at a local vegan restaurant, peeling garlic in the kitchen. In that moment he paused and for some reason experienced an intense connection with God. He was very content and filled with peace. It was a profound moment he would always remember.

Thomas continued to practice daily prayer. Centered in God, his insecurities and concerns for the future gradually lessoned and he began to focus on the present, learning to appreciate who he was. He continued with psychotherapy, but he was no longer dependent on it.

Spiritual Practice

(1) What is your center in life that holds and guides you?

(2) How do you nurture it?

(3) How might you invite God, Jesus, or the Holy Spirit to nurture your soul?

Prayer

God, I desire my life to be solidly centered in You and to be nurtured by Your presence. Help me to have joy in practicing a life of prayer.

How Marlin Discovered Herself in Brian and Reoriented Her Life

"Lord, may I know myself in order that I might know you."

—Augustine (354–430)

Marlin was a charming, unmarried 37-year-old accountant. She often questioned whether her present job was the right vocation for her. It lacked warmth and human involvement, but it gave her financial stability.

She used her money to travel but traveling made her feel rootless. She was able to deal with her external world but in her internal world, she could not hear the voice of God. She could no longer dismiss that deep feeling of emptiness. She decided to find a spiritual director to help her change her career and find an appropriate calling.

She compared her present life to a bus tour: A driver was taking her to different places while she was sitting in the comfortable seat of the bus. She experienced the world through the windows of the bus with no desire to get off to explore the world; she didn't listen to people crying; she was engaged in the world from a distance.

Whenever the world challenged her, she closed her ears and thought to herself, "I like staying where I am. I don't want to be bothered by anyone or anything. Leave me alone." An invisible thick wall stood between her and the world.

One day Marlin had an interesting encounter when she met a man named Brian who seemed to live an even more comfortable life than she did. Curiosity led her to be gradually drawn to him. At a cozy café, the two sipped tea and shared their views on life; they felt they had common ground and understood each other.

As Marlin got to know Brian's world, she was stunned by his behaviors. It seemed to her that he was totally dependent on others and that they existed to fulfill his needs. He didn't seem to take responsibility. Once Brian shared with her how his parents had neglected him in his childhood. Marlin thought that might be why he refused to be a responsible adult and acted much like a 5-year-old boy.

She felt anger towards him, "How can he be so irresponsible for his life?" Then she became sad. Where he had once been a colorful attractive box, he was now one of gray. When she opened the box, it was full of bitterness, hatred, blaming, and avoidance. She said goodbye to him, but the more she tried to ignore him, the stronger her emotional bonding with him became. She couldn't handle her obsession.

One day, she asked her friend, Jean, for advice. Jean had overcome a rough marriage with the help of much prayer. Her friend asked her, "Why don't you pray for your own healing rather than for his?" What surprising advice! Marlin started to pray for herself and occasionally included Brian as well.

Over time her prayer practice deepened and she perceived the kinds of changes she needed to make. She realized that Brian was mirroring her own wounded soul: She had been hurt as a child herself, raised by her grandmother and had felt abandoned by her parents. She now came to understand Brian's behaviors as a cry for help to escape his own misery.

Marlin felt his deep pain resonated with her own. Her feelings for Brian generated in her a love for God. During prayer, she came to realize that she had been running away from God and she knew she had developed a pattern of avoiding painful reality. But this time she turned around and said, "Here I am God, I will stop running away from You." She was awakening from a numbness towards the world.

She began to listen to her friends' pain, to talk with strangers, and to join prayer groups; she developed a concern for others. The wall that had separated her from the world was crumbling at last.

A few weeks later she visited Jean again and told her that she had submitted her resignation letter at work. She no longer had to escape from her authentic self.

Spiritual Practice

(1) How do you respond to unfairness or pain in your life? Do you accept it, bury it, avoid it, deny it, or run away from it?

(2) How have you expressed the pain you have experienced to people, society, and to God?

(3) Sit in quietness and observe what comes up in you. If you are ready, share your thoughts honestly with God.

Prayer

God, help me learn to respond to wounds in a way that promotes life and connection, rather than separation.

(4)

I Give Space.
Thus, I Receive Space

"When we are no longer able to change a situation, we are challenged to change ourselves."

—Viktor Frankl (1905–1997)

Sarah and her family were traumatized: Her beloved sister had just died of cancer, and more recently, her husband, Peter, was in a serious car accident.

Peter was gradually recovering physically, but he became depressed and was unable to go to work. He stopped shaving and meeting people. He grew more and more dependent on his wife, Sarah. He developed a fear that he was inadequate as a husband and father.

More unexpected incidents further stressed Sarah, including rashes that broke out all over her upper and lower back. She often cried and wondered when peace would return to her life. She belonged to a prayer group, had a spiritual director, and received advice from her immediate family, especially her mother. And yet, despite all the support, there seemed to be no treatment for her husband's depression.

Then an interesting opportunity was offered to her when she was invited to take a week-long trip to New York. There she would teach art students and present her own artwork at a gallery. Art was Sarah's life-long passion, but she was hesitant and concerned because of Peter's depression and increased dependency on her. He expected her to fill his needs and accompany him as much as she could, and she was also taking care of their two children. She wondered how he would handle daily chores and caring for the children all by himself. At the same time, she did not want to stop developing her professional life as an artist. "New York," she thought, "what an amazing opportunity!"

Despite her doubts, and after consulting with Peter, Sarah booked her flights. Before leaving, she was busy with preparations and hoped that she had prepared well enough so that Peter would find it easy to take care of the chores and children without her.

Sarah spent her week in the big city, very happy with her students and the realization of how much she enjoyed interacting with them. Her own artwork at the gallery was very well received and she felt stronger than she had in years. On her way back home, she was curious to see how her husband and her children had been doing without her.

When she arrived at home, her husband didn't complain at all. Rather, he was more actively taking care of himself, and she noticed something was happening inside of him: He had shaved, and she now felt that his handsome face was shinier. His long and untidy hair had been cut short and he looked young and charming. She asked him about how the week went. He simply said, "I asked the kids for help, saying to them, 'Daddy needs your help.' And they really listened to me, and we helped one another. Everything worked out well." As he spoke to Sarah, she felt new energy vibrating in him. How unexpected!

She was curious about what had brought about such a change. She had prayed for her husband so that he could handle the situation and his recovery from depression. Even though she couldn't figure it out fully, she glimpsed a possible answer for why he seemed to have changed: "Allow space for him."

She realized that in the future, she might need to give him more space to do things by himself.

Sarah visited her spiritual director and shared her experience, "My relationship with my husband was like two trees where one tree was leaning on the other. More and more the leaning tree lost its strength." She continued, "I need to trust him and his abilities, even if he may fall. I cannot hold his hands forever. Even if he falls, he may learn how to get up again." Then she paused and added, "I also began to look at myself. I need to trust myself more so that he can do things well without me."

A few weeks later, Sarah saw that her trip had initiated the opening of a door for Peter to trust himself, and through it she gained more space to enjoy her own freedom. In time her artwork grew in profound depth and the

lingering effects of Peter's depression became less fre-
quent and severe.

Spiritual Practice

(1) How do you respond to the needs of close family members, friends, or other people?

(2) What elements make you unable to see the potential
strength of others?

(3) What are some ways to cultivate trust in yourself or
others?

(4) Take 15 minutes of silent prayerful time and write the
words or draw some images that arise in you about
trust.

Prayer

Creator God, guide me as I discern which talents are mine
and which are those of others. Help me to trust You and
myself more so that I may be a co-creator with You. Let me
draw strength and beauty from within myself and others.

(5)

Julia's Inner Voice Leads Her Further

"For everything, there is a season, and a time for every matter under heaven: a time to be born, and a time to die; a time to plant, and a time to pluck up what is planted; a time to kill, and a time to heal; a time to break down, and a time to build up; a time to weep, and a time to laugh; a time to mourn, and a time to dance."

—Ecclesiastes 3:1–4

Julia grew up in a Catholic family. Since childhood, she had been athletic and loved fine art, especially painting. She studied fine art in college but saw no way to make that her livelihood, so she worked for an advertising company to try to live her artistic gift in that way. But it wasn't the same; her gift in fine art was different from the art and expression in advertising. On and off she complained about her life saying that it didn't go anywhere and felt incomplete.

She had a great sense of humor. As the youngest of four siblings, she often felt invisible and tried to get attention with humor. This continued even when she had become an adult. However, behind her humor, she felt deep sadness and mistrust for life.

Another stumbling block in Julia's growth was her beloved father's passing when she was still very young. Her mother, in her deep grief, became dependent on Julia and often expressed her sadness to her. When little Julia saw her mother suffering, she couldn't understand, "How can a good God take away my father from my mother and me when we need him so much?"

Julia also suffered other traumatic incidents. Once she fell from her favorite horse and was paralyzed for some time. By good fortune, she recovered and was able to live a normal life again. Another time she was found unconscious on the kitchen floor with dangerously low blood pressure and brought to the emergency room.

She felt as if the whole universe did not support her and that whenever she did not pay attention and control her environment, some sort of traumatic event would happen. She said, "I didn't think I could allow God to take responsibility for my life and my family members. Simply, I couldn't trust such an irresponsible God."

Her mistrust in God began to change when she slowly embraced the idea that when traumatic things happen, God was not to be blamed. Still, Julia continued to struggle with two opposing voices in herself: The voice of herself as a little girl and her adult voice. The little girl's voice kept her fixated on past experiences and made her feel fearful.

She developed a desire to control everything, attempting to plan every aspect of life to prevent another trauma. This fear kept her from moving on in her life. She was afraid of taking long trips away from home as she would much rather stay in her house. She worked on her home and created a beautiful garden. The house was her comfort zone where she could find peace, safety, and predictability.

The adult voice, however, kept challenging her to get out and pursue a courageous new life. But whenever she stood up to act on her adult voice, her siblings would criticize her for being too adventurous and her child's voice would take over.

One evening she had a severe pain in her sacrum and her hip. She could barely walk. It seemed her pain was telling her that it was time to take some action.

Julia visited her friend Kimberly who was a practitioner of holistic alternative medicine. Kimberly listened to her story and then asked Julia, "What would be a way for that courageous adult Julia to guide the fearful little girl, Julia?" Julia replied, "I don't need to be ruled by the voice of the little girl anymore. Now it's time for the adult voice to guide me." This was a profound insight for her.

Then, while she was gardening one afternoon, she heard a very clear voice from within speaking firmly to her: "You need to face the truth. You can do it. You are a capable and powerful woman." It was her adult voice. It might have been God's response to her ongoing prayers, she thought. She adopted that voice as her real self.

Changes began to take place. She began to believe that if she prayed to God in her adult voice, those prayers might be answered. She had read in the Bible the story of how Jesus had raised Lazarus from death, but she realized that certain things could not be answered, such as her prayers as a little girl for her father to come back. As a grown woman, she could pray for realistic things.

Her husband was offered a new job that required him to move to another state. He was delighted with the opportunity since it would mean a return to the area of his birth and an exciting new chapter in life. Julia, however, was sad because she didn't want to leave everything behind—her beloved house, friends, and her siblings nearby. But she also did not want to remain stuck—and safe.

After praying with God, she thought that this might be the time to take that courageous step to leave her comfort zone. She didn't know what she would do in their new place while her husband would be off to work. Reluctantly she began looking for jobs there herself.

Surprisingly, she got an opportunity to apply for a job in the same city where her husband worked. She had little expectation but after a single interview, the door opened for her. She said, "We were praying for a long time for job doors to open. It is not a coincidence that now we both have new work and even in the same city."

Julia and her husband moved to the new state. At an unexpected time, the truth within herself led her to a new opportunity.

Spiritual Practice

(1) Do you feel that you are stuck in your life?

(2) What are the hindrances that block your life from moving forward?

(3) What is your image of God? Is it freeing or is it an obstacle?

(4) Set aside some time to pray over your fears and desires.

Prayer

God, You make new things possible. Help me to discern Your voice from mine or others. Give me the courage to respond to Your voice within me and to take a new path in life with less fear.

(6)

A Letter That is Bringing Joy

*"In Christ God was reconciling the world to Godself,
not counting their trespasses against them, and
entrusting the message of reconciliation to us."*

—2 Corinthians 5:19

Jin lived in the southern part of South Korea near his mother and his younger sister who lived in a small old house that had been paid off. One day, as part of a new housing project, the local city government notified them that the old houses in their neighborhood might be demolished.

Leaving behind many memorable items, his mother and sister rushed to move to a nearby apartment. The city eventually cancelled the construction project and yet they did not return to the old house, since they now enjoyed the comfort and amenities of the new apartment.

The old house remained vacant.

Jin was also facing challenges of his own with financial troubles and a possible divorce from his wife. He wanted to return to his mother's empty old house but there were significant obstacles and emotional wounds that he had not faced. For instance, he had never felt his mother's love for him and as a result, he expected more love from his wife. As a result, his marriage ended bitterly, and he felt the pain deeply. His relationship with his daughter was also worsening and they had a hard time simply speaking to one another.

Fortunately, he soon found an engaging job at a start-up company. The 8-hour night-shift work was not easy, but he enjoyed the effort of assembling auto accessories. He was usually there by himself, listening to Christian radio music, sermons, hymns, and personal testimonies. In these solitary hours, he was stimulated to reflect on his own life.

An important change began to take place in his life. He joined an early-morning prayer service after work and laid out his concerns in front of God, asking for His guidance and protection for his only daughter and his now-former wife. He regretted his divorce and realized how it—*how he*—hurt everyone deeply, including himself. He asked God for both forgiveness and to heal his daughter, his ex-wife, and himself.

As time passed by, he made many repairs to the old house: He fixed the broken plumbing and leaking ceilings and added steel stairs to climb to the top of the roof; he trimmed the wildly growing pomegranate tree in the small yard and was reminded of his childhood. He developed a very special affection for the old family house: It gave him a private space in which he felt peace.

Despite his growth, Jin still felt the deep sense of hurt with his mother, made worse every time she pointed out his mistakes.

One afternoon, the mailman delivered a letter addressed to his mother. Apparently, he had been trying to deliver it personally to her many times over the last several years. Jin opened the letter and found information from the Korean Social Security Administration (SSA) about additional benefits for his mother. He thought, "How wonderful for my mother!" In addition to his painful emotions, he had been harboring guilty feelings about not being able to support her more financially.

The letter required several steps to make her eligible for these benefits. The first requirement was that his mother should be physically present at the SSA. The second requirement was more unusual: She needed to use a traditional rubber stamp to inscribe her name instead of a personal handwritten signature. In Korea, people once used a personalized stamp as their signature. But these stamps had long been discontinued. He thought that it might be quite a challenge to find someone who would still make such signature stamps with so few in use. He prayed to God to help his mother.

On a sunny Friday morning, Jin took his feeble 80-year-old mother to the appointment. She was happy over the good news about the additional money coming to her from social security. Afterward, he held her hand and guided her steps to her favorite noodle place where they enjoyed lunch. She told him stories about his grand-parents and his childhood, and afterward they went to the bank and opened an account for her in her own name—her first. As a wife, she had been dependent upon her husband's financial identity.

Jin still needed to solve the challenge of finding a stamp inscriber. He came upon a small old store with a "Rubber Stamps" sign and felt that perhaps it was God's providence to lead him there. The store's inscriber turned out to be a close friend of Jin's daughter—truly miraculous! Back home, Jin reflected, "What a lovely and unforgettable day, especially to have helped, and been able to help, through my prayer."

A few months later, Jin saw that a check from Social Security had been deposited into his mother's bank account. He phoned her and said, "Mom, your money has arrived." He could hear the delight in her voice, "Thank you, my son." For a few moments, he was silent, and then he felt gratitude to God who had listened to his inner struggles and encouraged him to resume a warm relationship with his mother.

Jin said to himself in a quiet voice, "God really listens."

Spiritual Practice

(1) Have you had a special experience that eased your worries and concerns?

(2) How did it happen?

(3) How did you feel the presence of God in that incident?

(4) You might take your concerns to God, lay them out in front of God, and sense how God might be guiding you.

Prayer

God, as we lay our cares and concerns out in front of You, we thank You for listening to them. Please open our spiritual eyes to recognize Your presence in our daily struggle.

(7)

What Elaine Was Really Searching for

"For where your treasure is, there will your heart be also."

—Luke 12:34

Elaine and John met in college in a club for medical students assigned to the same project. While working as a team, Elaine observed John's sincere and genuine heart as he cared for patients and others.

John told Elaine that he once thought to serve God as a priest, but his path led him to study medicine and become a doctor. As a devout Catholic, John's mother, Mary, wished he would have become a priest.

Elaine felt John's special attention and affection for her. She was attracted to him as well, but she didn't know how to express her affection for him. Though they never dated, Elaine kept him close in her heart. His warmth and deep caring for others soothed her soul. She wondered where his caring nature came from.

Eventually, John got married to someone else. Elaine and John still met occasionally, along with other college friends. John's life seemed perfect outwardly: he had children, was a respected doctor, and had a beautiful wife. But he never looked happy. Elaine wondered how he was really doing. She still saw a treasure in him which she could not explain.

One night John's mother Mary appeared in Elaine's dream. She looked concerned for her son. Holding Elaine's hands, Mary asked her for a special favor, "Elaine, you should not let John go." What a strange dream it was! She couldn't understand the meaning of the dream and soon forgot about it. Still, on and off, Elaine held John in her prayers, asking that his soul may find peace in God. Often when she prayed for John, she somehow felt close to Jesus.

One rainy morning, she was in her office, looking out the window. Her friend Nancy, a close friend of John's as well, phoned to tell her that John's mother had had a heart attack and died. She invited Elaine to the funeral service and asked whether they could attend together.

Elaine remembered the smell of fresh whole grain bread and the taste of sweet peach pie that Mary would bake. She sighed, "Unbelievable, Mary is not here anymore."

Elaine and Nancy attended Mary's funeral service. A gloomy atmosphere surrounded everything. Elaine watched John sobbing quietly. He looked like a bird, wet in the rain, with feathers soaked. She wondered what he was going through with his mother's sudden death.

She had another dream several months after Mary's funeral service. This time the dream was about her own funeral service. A black ribbon encircled her picture. Although she was dead, Elaine wore a long black robe, greeting each visitor at the entrance door of her house and guiding them into the living room. Her friends were talking about how Elaine cared for them and how much they missed her.

John, for whom she still had loving feelings, arrived late. After he greeted her, he tied his shoestrings and looked as if he was ready to leave again. Disappointed that his visit was so short, she asked him, "Where are you going, John? You just arrived." He looked at her and said, "I am leaving you. You don't love me anymore." When she heard this, she felt sad, but she couldn't keep him from leaving and watched as he went out the door. Then the dream ended.

Later she shared it with her older sister Judy who knew that to Elaine, John always seemed unhappy. Elaine said, "That dream is very symbolic to me, Judy. What he said in the dream was right. Despite his sadness, I feel John's deep and profound warmth. I always wanted to know where that warmth originated. Like in the dream I was afraid that he would leave me before I discovered his secret. Now I know. There is in John a Divine light. It is Jesus in him who I now realize I dearly love. It is not John as a sweetheart. John is a stepping stone to lead me to Jesus. I feel grateful for the dream."

Elaine looked up as if she let a small bird in her heart freely fly away.

Spiritual Practice

(1) What is the treasure that you cherish most in your heart?

(2) Pay attention to your dreams or situations that recur. What do they say to you? Can you give them a title or a name?

(3) Where do you feel God's guidance in an unfulfilled dream or desire?

(4) Set aside some time to quiet your mind and listen to your inner wisdom. What images or messages come to you?

Prayer

God, Consoler, Revealer, Liberator, help us to understand how or when You speak to us. Open our hearts so that we may listen to our inner wisdom.

(8)

A Spiritual Companionship

"Now on that same day, two of them were going to a village called Emmaus, about seven miles from Jerusalem, and talking with each other about all these things that had happened. While they were talking and discussing, Jesus himself came near and went with them."

—Luke 24:13–15

Adelina, a preschool teacher, had beautiful and abundant red curly hair. To her, her hair was the symbol of her beauty. But then, Adelina noticed she was losing a handful of hair every time she washed it. Afraid that she might lose her boyfriend (he loved her hair), she called a friend of her sister's, a doctor of Oriental medicine named Nicole, to see whether herbs could prevent hair loss.

During her first office visit, Adelina told Nicole about her medical history. She also shared her inner conflicts, particularly her low self-esteem and depression. She said that she was seeing a psychiatrist and taking anti-depressant medications, and her family was very supportive. While Nicole listened attentively, Adelina realized that her real concern was neither her hair loss nor her beauty. Instead, she had disguised her fears: What she really wanted was to live a joyful life. This was an incredible revelation!

A month or so after her conversation with Nicole, Adelina separated from her boyfriend who also suffered from depression. The breakup triggered a relapse of her own depression, and she was admitted to a psychiatric unit. Adelina's older sister went to see Nicole and asked her if she could visit Adelina, thinking that she would like a visit from her. They soon arranged a meeting for her at the psychiatric hospital.

During their visit Adelina shared how depression gave her negative thoughts while Nicole quietly listened without judgment. Adelina appreciated Nicole's visit very much and went to see her a few days later after she was discharged.

The treatment Adelina received relaxed her and made her feel more peaceful; she felt Nicole understood and sincerely cared for her. During her treatment, Adelina shared how negative, harsh voices within herself caused her to have sleepless, anxious nights. Despite the support of her family, friends, and fellow teachers, it was an exceedingly difficult time for Adelina.

Nicole felt Adelina's suffering and acknowledged her pain, "This is really rough for you, Adelina. I know you are trying so hard. I wonder if you could add a more spiritual approach to your support. What do you know about Jesus and how he healed people?"

"I know he was a good man who helped and healed people. But I don't really know him. Would you tell me more?"

Adelina was eager to learn about Jesus. She wanted so much to be healed. Nicole brought a Bible from her bookshelf and asked Adelina to read a healing story about a man who lived among tombs. Jesus had made an effort to see this isolated and lonely man who lived in agony and came to heal him.

"How great of Jesus to visit this suffering man, and to heal him," said Adelina. She then asked Nicole, "How can I know Jesus personally?"

Nicole suggested to her, "You invite Jesus into your heart and ask him to dwell in you and be your companion." Adelina didn't understand how to invite Jesus into her heart. Nicole offered a song: "Into my heart, into my heart, come into my heart, Lord Jesus. Come in today, come into stay, come into my heart, Lord Jesus."*

Adelina felt something warm touch her emotionally; she was very grateful for the song.

Adelina occasionally felt peaceful in this new spiritual world. She found a Christian group of praise near her school, and she often sat alone in the corner of the worship room quietly. She would join the others in singing in the circle and eventually, with the help of medication

---

*Harry D. Clarke, 1924; sung by Kwang-hee Park in a video on StoriesOfSpiritualHealing (dot) com

and her music, she returned to her work as a teacher with small children. Still, despite the intermittent feelings of peace, Adelina suffered from bouts of severe depression. She was terrorized by an inner voice that threatened her life. She was especially fearful when she heard that voice while she was alone.

At the end of the year, Adelina's sister called Nicole to share the news that Adelina's depression had caused her to take her own life. Her family was in deep grief. Nicole fought back her tears, "I am so sorry to hear that. It is so sad. And she had just been so happy to return to teaching children again." Adelina's sister invited Nicole to the memorial service.

The service was very emotional and touching. Adelina's father was so distraught that he was unable to read the letter he had written to his daughter and guests were moved by the collection of Adelina's belongings—small wildflowers, tiny stones, and small knitted dolls. Adelina had loved and cared for small things, just as she had cared for her small preschoolers; perhaps in the end it had been the world that was simply too big for her.

After the service, there was a farewell party for her family, friends, schoolteachers, and neighbors. Adelina had occasionally invited her neighbors to share meals, and this gathering with its food, quiet music, and mingling together was Adelina's final gift for her loved ones.

Adelina had left Nicole a note which her family shared with her at the gathering. It was signed, "A true healer. Love, Adelina." Nicole wished she had spent more time with her and had checked in more often.

Adelina's sister and her family truly appreciated the spiritual guidance Nicole had offered her. They knew that it took a considerable amount of time and attention for a person caught by the challenges of depression to find ease from his or her difficulties by way of spiritual healing.

Spiritual Practice

(1) Have you experienced the need for spiritual companionship in times of struggle?

(2) Whom do you want to invite as spiritual companions on your journey? How would you like to invite him or her?

(3) Sit in silence. Listen to your thoughts, images, or emotions together with the spiritual companion you have invited. When would you say that your spiritual journey awakened and healed you?

(4) How might you reach out to someone in deep despair?

Prayer

Jesus Christ, I want to live my life fully and joyfully. Help me to love myself as I am. Be my spiritual companion. I invite you into my heart. Stay with me.

(9)

The Night Jesus Visited

"A week later his disciples were again in the house, and Thomas was with them. Although the doors were shut, Jesus came and stood among them and said, 'Peace be with you.'"

—John 20:26

Jacob was studying theology. He enjoyed his relationship with his girlfriend, Anna. The time came when he felt he needed to decide if he wanted to marry her but he was very conflicted inside.

He always felt her presence when things mattered the most. One of those moments was when he helped his beloved 93-year-old grandfather to the airport for a long flight to visit family. Jacob imagined to someday introduce Anna to his grandfather and how special that would be.

Another occasion was at his brother's wedding when his family was celebrating the new couple with singing and dancing. Jacob wished Anna could be there. Whenever there were important events in his life, he felt her spiritual presence and couldn't ignore their deep spiritual connection. This led him back to her whenever he felt he should let her go.

And yet, several issues still prevented him from saying "Yes." As a Presbyterian Christian Anna gave ten percent of her income to the church. He thought that giving half of that was more than enough; her strong practice in tithing and her intimate relationship with Jesus challenged him. Unlike Anna, he had not developed a personal relationship with Jesus. He respected Jesus as a moral teacher and as a friend, but no more. Despite these differences, he knew that he was ready to consider marriage with her.

Jacob received an opportunity for a temporary job as a secretary in a law firm overseas. While there, he stayed at a Catholic seminary dormitory for three months. On the first floor was a chapel and its architectural simplicity attracted him: the room was round and sparse with white walls, grey pews, a few candles spread around, and a flower or two. Next to an altar stood a cross with the crucified body of Jesus. Jacob spent hours praying in this beautiful and peaceful chapel. He was discerning his relationship with Anna.

Every day he sat in front of the cross in silence; sometimes two or three hours passed while he was deep in prayer. He proposed one question to God: "Should I marry Anna, or not?" He really wanted to listen to the spirit of God and yield his heart to God. He specifically committed one full year to prayerfully discerning marriage with Anna, marking his calendar with what he thought he heard emerging within himself from deep down. Gradually more and more calendar days showed, "Yes." Initially, the marks were split evenly, half "Yes" and half "No."

One night, around 1 a.m. he was sleeping when he suddenly felt that the Jesus on the cross in the chapel came walking up the stairs and down the hallway towards Jacob's room. Jacob thought, "What am I going to do?" His body felt very heavy, as if he were frozen. He couldn't move. He breathed deeply, lying face-down on his stomach. "The door is locked," he realized, but that didn't matter to Jesus as He walked right through it and sat down on the edge of Jacob's bed. Jacob felt Jesus laying one hand on his back and the other on his head and Jacob felt deep love. Jesus then said, "It is okay to give only five percent as a tithe." Some moments later Jesus left, walked back down the hallway, down the stairs, and returned to the cross in the chapel.

What was this? Jacob was amazed. He remained flat in bed and didn't move. He continued breathing very deeply and eventually fell back asleep.

In the morning—and for several days to come—Jacob was still amazed. What *was* this? He was bewildered—but he also felt deeply understood by Jesus. It was a very good feeling.

Jacob kept this special, personal spiritual encounter in his heart for a long time. He was certain that it was something different from a dream. But what was it? A vision? A professor in a class about mystical experiences suggested that it was a visitation, and this made sense to Jacob; it was a visitation, not a dream, and not a vision. His mind now had an answer, and a sense of understanding. Jacob no longer needed to analyze what he experienced; he was now able to purely enjoy the experience and be grateful.

Six weeks later Jacob finished his year of discernment over his relationship with Anna. Nervous but ready, and still overseas, he called her and asked, "Anna, will you marry me?" Anna said, "Are you proposing to me? Are you really? Yes, Jacob, I will!"

Over the next few years, Jacob's questioning mind and conflicting emotions continued to trouble him. At times he would call out to God, "Help me! You told me to marry Anna!" In his struggles, he committed himself to God—and vice versa, "I am committing God to me."

Four years later he was able to visit the chapel again, this time together with Anna. He was so glad to show it to her and see that nothing had changed: the beauty of its simplicity, Jesus on the cross. Jacob then laid himself face-down flat on the floor. Jesus said to him, "Listen to God. You made the right decision." Jacob was greatly relieved and very grateful to Jesus.

Spiritual Practice

(1) Have you had a special spiritual experience?

(2) How do you explain it?

(3) How has that spiritual experience changed or shaped your life? Has it been positive or negative?

Prayer

Jesus, thank you for accepting me as I am and helping me to develop a close relationship with you.

(10)

Jinny's Inner Voice Gives Her Heart Peace

"The purposes in the human mind are like deep water, but the intelligent will draw them out."

—Proverbs 20:5

Jinny worked as a pharmacist for over seven years. She often doubted her career choice and wondered if it was the right path for her. She grew up in a Christian family where the influence of her parents was strong, and it was their choice of pharmacist as her profession.

Over time Jinny considered becoming a massage therapist because it had always impressed her how Jesus healed others through touch. She wondered whether her job in the pharmacy satisfied her desire to heal. Critical thoughts within her grew and challenged her to quit her job. She was confused.

Jinny also liked books and sometimes she spent entire days reading. She read about spirituality and self-discovery and wanted to develop her authentic self which she believed God had given her.

At one time, Jinny had joined a spiritual program to help her examine herself. However, the reading assignments overwhelmed her, and she could not finish the program. The leader of the course recommended to her to seek a spiritual director that would help her in discerning her career and her desire for deeper spirituality.

When Jinny found a spiritual director, she talked about her doubts with her profession. Jinny explained that her external qualifications met all the requirements for her job: education, licensing, and experience. She was doing well and there were no complaints from customers or her supervisor but the voices from within her were powerfully accusative: "You are not precise enough; not detail-oriented; you don't follow the most recent scientific knowledge. You are not an adequate medical professional." She also told her spiritual director that if she were to leave the pharmacy, a more-qualified person could better serve the customers and the company.

The spiritual director, Phoebe, listened to her and raised a question, "I wonder where these negative voices are coming from?" Jinny realized that the critical views about herself didn't come from her supervisors or colleagues, but rather from within herself. At that moment, another voice emerged: "Jinny, don't be so serious. Forget your work. Enjoy your life and have fun. Life is short. You are doing fine at your workplace. Live a comfortable life."

She was left entirely confused. Which voice should she trust?

In response, her spiritual director suggested that they sit in silence and see what other images or thoughts might arise. During the silence, Jinny began to feel a deep joy. She remembered the moment when she finished her years of education. The pharmacy program was so rigorous that she often questioned her capacity and wanted to give up. She would pray, "Jesus, help me to get through just this one semester." In the end, when she finally completed the program, she felt that it was a sign of God's desire to support her.

Jinny opened her eyes and said, "It came to me that God has been with me throughout my career and has guided me." Tears came down her cheeks; it was as if God knew her struggling heart. The spiritual director replied, "I am glad to hear that you feel God has guided your studies. You also said that you are doing quite well at work. What do you think helps you most in your job?" Jinny quickly responded, "My smile and my kindness. I think I also have good social skills. My colleagues say that I create a warm, supportive, and fun working environment and I haven't made any mistakes. There was one incident, but the medicine was misplaced, and we found it the next day. My manager told me that since I've been working there, the pharmacy's income has nearly doubled." Jinny thought more for a moment... "Wow! This meditation has helped me to become aware of all this!"

Jinny could not stop smiling and she became aware of a voice within her that nurtured her like living water, washing away her old negative thoughts. She was able to restore the caring voice within. She had not felt that she was on the right path for the longest time and now she did.

Jinny continued her spiritual direction sessions once per month. She explored how she might incorporate her desire to heal into her career and she soon discovered that the way she cared for her customers could be an expression of her faith.

A few months later, Jinny was offered the opportunity to host a small show on a Christian radio program. She encouraged people to examine their faith and how it might be meaningful in their work and careers. She felt much more at ease at the pharmacy and in her career.

Spiritual Practice

(1) Sit in silence and listen to your inner voices. What images or words arise in you about an issue you are struggling with?

(2) Do these inner voices support, dismiss or perhaps negate your experiences with God accepting you as you are?

(3) How might you draw upon your inner wisdom to nurture your soul?

Prayer

God, help me to find the living waters within me that refresh and nourish my spirit—that I may live my calling.

(11)

A Holy Mark

"Remember, then, that you received a spiritual seal, the spirit of wisdom and understanding, the spirit of knowledge and reverence, the spirit of holy fear. Keep safe what you received. God the Father sealed you, Christ the Lord strengthened you and sent the Spirit into your hearts as the pledge of what is to come."

—Ambrose (c. 340–397)

Nathan, a Jewish nurse, valued friendship. He had a special connection with his young German Christian colleague Steven. They worked in the same hospital and enjoyed talking about life and meaning.

When there were special family occasions, Nathan invited Steven and his wife to join him. He liked to welcome friends and spend celebratory occasions with his family at home. His children had grown up and two of them were now with families of their own. He invited Steven and his wife for Passover, Thanksgiving, and his granddaughter's naming ceremony. He felt that they were part of his family.

During one gathering at Passover, Nathan explained the Jewish holiday's meaning to Steven. When Steven entered the house and tried to close the door, Nathan said, "Please keep the door open to welcome the prophet Elijah so that he would bless this house." The same evening Nathan introduced his friend Adam, a Holocaust survivor, to Steven. They quickly engaged in a conversation and Adam asked questions about Steven's parents and grandparents. Wearing a big smile, Adam invited Steven to visit his house to show him his personal library. Steven smiled and nodded. Nathan was happy to see the two getting to know each other.

Another occasion was for Nathan's grandson's Brit Milah, or the ceremony for the covenant of circumcision. Again, Nathan opened his house and invited his friends from work, the synagogue, and elsewhere. This time, Steven's wife came by herself explaining, "Steven is down with the flu." Nathan appreciated that Steven's wife would come by herself.

At the ceremony, Nathan wore his Kippah and a Talit, a blue-silver prayer shawl. He greeted his guests with drinks and then sat with his grandson on his lap while the guests took pictures. In one corner of the house, Nathan saw Steven's wife talking with his friends.

Gradually the guests became quiet and the rabbi began the Brit Milah ceremony. The physician Nathan had invited began the circumcision as the baby cried. Steven's wife, standing in the corner, saw how both parents had tears in their eyes. She was reflecting on how this was a sign of the covenant among Jewish people and their dedication to God, remembering her own covenant with God. She felt that for her, Jesus' death on the cross was a holy mark on her heart.

When the physician had finished, there was a profound moment of silence; a holy moment as if time itself had stopped. Nathan had observed Steven's wife keenly watching the ceremony and thought that as a Christian she might have read about the tradition in the Bible. The celebration concluded with singing and a triple blessing over the child; Nathan felt a deep connection, "I hope someday the baby will appreciate his everlasting bond with God."

While the food was being served, Steven's wife approached Nathan's son-in-law, the baby's father. His father was a pastor, so he had grown up in a Christian family. She said to him, "This is the way for Jews to remember their covenant with God." Nathan felt she might connect with the baby's father as a Christian. She said, "Christians believe they have holy marks on their hearts." Nathan added, "Circumcision is a symbol of bonding with God."

Nathan prayed that the child would indeed develop a close relationship with God. He felt close to his friends and family as they shared this special, holy moment.

A couple of years later Nathan retired and invited Steven and his wife to a big retirement gathering. He enjoyed having time for his grandchildren and hiking with friends. Nathan continued his conversations with Steven, often sharing wisdom from his experiences in life.

Spiritual Practice

(1) What is your holy mark that reminds you of who you are in relationship to God?

(2) How do you appreciate or cherish the holy experiences of others that remind them of who they are?

(3) Take time to feel the presence of others who give you meaning and are part of who you are. Hold them in your prayers for their precious presence in your life.

Prayer

God, thank You for reminding me of who I am—a holy being—whether my holy mark is visible or not.

(12)

Reunion

*"I praise you, for I am fearfully and wonderfully
made. Wonderful are your works; that I know very
well."*

—Psalm 139:14

Laura was a student in a Ph.D. program. In one of
her courses, she received an essay assignment
on self-development. When she thought about the essay,
an assignment about identity, the first thought that came
to her mind was, "I wish I was born a man." She was not
surprised; indeed, she thought that it might in fact be her
deep, unconscious desire to be a man.

As a single Asian woman, Laura felt that in the patriarchal society in which she grew up it was unfair that a
woman was judged by her husband's status. She had decided to raise her own social status by pursuing a professional career in teaching.

When Laura reached forty, she considered getting
married. She dated several men but soon realized that

her pursuit of higher education was an obstacle to marriage because men felt threatened by her education. Laura sighed, "If I were a man in a Ph.D. program, many women would be in line to marry me!"

Laura remained determined, and instead of seeking marriage, she delved further into her studies. "I want to be an independent woman with my own career, not be dependent on some man," she thought. She didn't even give much attention to her appearance to be more attractive. Courses on feminism helped her find ways to raise her own voice. And yet, despite her determination to be an independent woman, she still felt conflicted with a deep longing to have her own family and was now caught between her desire to marry and her professional goals.

When Laura thought about marriage, she found herself feeling stressed and depressed. As she faced her loneliness, she opened herself to interact more with the families of fellow students, many of them pastors. She deepened her own deep prayer life and cared more for others. She also joined a prayer group with other Ph.D. students where she learned that married students often struggled with the dual burden of financial responsibility for their family and the demands of rigorous study.

The prayer group became a life-line for Laura. It helped her to accept being single while studying. The weekly meals she was having with the prayer group eased her loneliness and she felt that she had a warm extended spiritual family. Her continuous prayer life both personal and with others slowly brought about an inner transformation.

One day while she was driving to the market, Laura thought of the book that she was carefully reading, Betty Friedan's *"Feminine Mystique."* She learned about the many layers of social expectations that held women back and realized that she grew up with the flawed belief that a strong woman's life will be rough, and her happiness dependent upon a man's love. As she was thinking about her life, the image of a spider came to her. The spider was caught in the entangled threads of a cobweb and though it tried to get out, it kept getting caught in other threads. That spider was like herself. Laura began to cry, even sob, "Oh Lord, this is how so many women experience themselves. They don't know how to break these stifling, culturally habituated expectations and even taboos." In this moment of tears and realization, she formed a strong sense of solidarity with other women who were caught in the same patriarchal social structures.

Laura was overwhelmed by this self-awakening and yet she didn't know how to express her new realization. She had a good friend who was studying feminism who listened to her for many hours. She suggested that Laura write down or draw her feelings, so Laura wrote poems and drew pictures. Finally, a series of dreams gave her more insight; one in particular where a big ax broke apart her bathtub which was buried under the ground. After this dream she felt as if her old self was broken.

A few days after this revelation she dreamt again. This time Laura was in a building and a person was chasing her. The person wore a black hood and she couldn't see their face. She saw an exit sign and ran towards it as fast as she could to get out of the building and away from the pursuer.

And yet as she ran, Laura suddenly had a strong desire to see the person who was running after her. She turned around, grabbed the person by the arm, and asked, "Who are you? Why do you keep chasing me? Let me see your face!" With a brush of her hand, she removed the hood. Strange, the face was *very* familiar to her. She said gently, "Your face is so familiar to me; come, I will buy you new clothes and shave your mustache. I will be your friend." She held the person's arm tight.

When Laura woke up she didn't understand the dream, thinking perhaps that it might mean she would soon meet her future spouse. While she was journaling about the dream, however, it dawned on her that the person chasing her was in fact a part of herself—her dismissed, neglected and buried self as a woman; her inner self, so utterly familiar, had become nearly masculine and represented with a mustache.

She felt so sorry for herself; the beautiful, kind, and gentle woman she was had been buried under her desire to be an independent and strong woman. She had pushed her vulnerable, gentle, soft self into the shadow. She sobbed and said, "I am sorry, I am so sorry." That night Laura hugged the abandoned part of herself in her arms. She said, "I will never again dismiss you."

The dream was a turning point for Laura. For the first time in her adult life, she deeply appreciated being a woman, a gift from God.

A year later, Laura met a man in a self-reflective ministry group. He fully embraced her and recognized her as a unique woman. Laura combined both her marriage with

her professional career, and neither was subordinate to
the other.

Spiritual Practice

(1) Do you have an unsolved problem or recurring theme
in your life that you need to face?

(2) How have you dealt with it until now?

(3) Have you experienced some form of self-transforma-
tion with the problem, and have you reconciled it?

Prayer

God, help me to own my whole being and not dismiss un-
recognized parts in me. Guide me to cherish the process of
transformation as I deal with my issue.

(13)

Sometimes the Real Gift Comes from Someone You Never Even Thought of

"Beloved, I pray that all may go well with you and that you may be in good health, just as it is well with your soul."

—3 John 1:2

George worked in an organization that advocated for non-violent solutions to local and global conflicts.

This year he wanted to celebrate his birthday with his close friends in his small house. He invited Matt, a Ph.D. candidate in theology; Tomas and Yolanda, an activist couple; and Adam, a lawyer for the local city government. Adam used to be a Bible study leader, but then he developed a rebellious attitude towards traditional Christian faith. For some time, he wanted to be a pastor, but he viewed himself as unqualified because he found his thoughts often scattered and confused.

Adam also suffered from depression. Some days he would stay at home, hiding and reading the whole day. He felt that his identity as a man had not fully develop, perhaps because he never felt a nurturing connection with his father. He was a very sensitive child and he often felt lonely. Adam had once told George that in his childhood God was the only friend he could really talk to.

Adam arrived early to help George prepare the birthday dinner. They set the table with wine and water glasses, plates, and George's favorite decorations: a white tablecloth, yellow tulips, and red candles.

George opened the front windows wide. He enjoyed feeling the city atmosphere through his windows—a Hispanic supermarket, cars, and the colors of a changing traffic signal. Adam noticed that all kinds of people, many poor, walked by on the sidewalk. George said, "I often think to myself that every one of them has their unique story."

Jazz music played on the radio as his other friends arrived; one brought a bottle of wine, another an apple pie, and everyone brought birthday gifts.

George had prepared a special dish for the evening: salmon with pineapple and an arugula salad. They all cheered to the sound of glasses clinking and the sounds of the "Happy birthday" song made him feel like the center of the day. During dinner, they enjoyed conversations on faith and practice and politics.

George then heard a knock on the door and a small Latino man stood outside requesting food. George thought perhaps he was homeless and he asked his friends whether the man could join them at the dinner table. They all responded, "Of course," and welcomed the man who introduced himself as Roberto.

He listened to the conversation as Adam was leading a discussion on the Bible. At one point, Adam stood up and excused himself. Roberto asked if he could sing a song in appreciation for the warm dinner. He said, "I will wait first for your pastor to return," thinking that they were having a Bible study group and that Adam was the pastor.

After Adam returned to his chair, Roberto said, "Thank you, pastor, for welcoming me here. If you allow, I will give testimony to Jesus and I want to sing for you all." George's friends smiled and said, "Yes, pastor, we want to hear his testimony."

Adam's face lit up: "Please, go ahead." Roberto stood next to his chair and with his right hand on his heart, he sang, "My Jesus, I love Thee," and tears were in his eyes.

A short while later he left. There was a moment of silence.

This unexpected guest was a special gift for George and his friends. The man had touched their souls, especially Adam's. Adam felt as if God knew his unfulfilled wish and inner conflict.

Spiritual Practice

(1) Have you experienced an unexpected recognition that overrode your feelings about yourself?

(2) How did it happen? How did you feel?

(3) Is there any person in your life now that needs special
attention from you?

Prayer

God, thank You for reminding us of being Your beloved
children, regardless of any shortcomings. Often, we don't
see how precious we are, and we need Your reminders.

(14)

How a Fairly Inappropriate Laugh Led to a Feeling of Acceptance

"Humor is the affectionate communication of insight."

—Leo Rosten (1908–1997)

Guenther attended a Unitarian Universalist church and created a Bible study group there. He also taught American history at a local university. Living in California, Guenther enjoyed hiking, jogging on the beach, and joining conferences and workshops for self-development.

A new couple, Albert and Jennifer, visited the Unitarian Universalist church and joined Guenther's Bible study. Over time, Albert and Guenther became good friends, discussing religion, society, and politics, and they would send each other links to newspaper articles. When they got together, they would occasionally burst into laughter in the middle of a conversation. Guenther felt that Albert and

Jennifer were more than friends to him. In fact, Jennifer often called him "Uncle Guenther."

One Saturday morning, Albert called Guenther to see if he wanted to meet that evening because Jennifer would be away at a revival meeting. He only needed to stop at the church first to deliver food for the meeting.

When Albert and Guenther arrived at the church, a female pastor was just about to finish a prophetic ministry. About 30 people in the audience were listening to her speak.

Albert brought in the food and the two men were invited to join the meal. After the dinner break, the pastor continued to preach. Guenther was curious about the people attending. Why did they have such a passion for the gospel? Everyone looked very attentive and quiet. Albert and Guenther were the only non-Asians present and although they couldn't understand the language, they tried to understand what was going on.

Suddenly Guenther looked at Albert and said in a low voice, "The pastor looks like a toadstool mushroom." She was wearing a red dress with white dots scattered all over it. Both men immediately blushed and fell into uncontrollable laughter, trying to hide it behind their hands. Guenther's mother had often warned him about the poisonous nature of the toadstool mushroom. He was so embarrassed at his laughter that he left the room.

Albert followed him. He, too, could not stop laughing; it kept coming like waves upon the ocean. Guenther crossed the street and sat in a café and when Albert saw him from a distance and their eyes met, the laughter just would not stop. Albert put his hands on his belly, it hurt from all the laughing, and Guenther was shaking; they could barely contain themselves.

It took an hour before the two men were able to return quietly to the lecture room. They wanted to apologize. Laughter, however, again overwhelmed them. Finally, the pastor paused her sermon and asked Guenther what was making them laugh so much. Guenther shared how her dress reminded him of the mushroom his mother would warn him about as a child. Hearing this, everyone in the room laughed. The pastor was not upset, in fact, she joined in the laughing. The whole room was filled with the joyful sounds.

Guenther was impressed by the pastor and the people in the church. He felt that their response was generous and that they understood him. That experience of acceptance made Guenther feel at home.

The revival meeting was an unexpected spiritual gift that refreshed Guenther's soul. He felt at home in God, beyond language and cultural boundaries.

Spiritual Practice

(1) Have you had an experience that lightened your seriousness?

(2) When you laugh with others, what kind of spiritual feelings do you have? A sense of connectedness perhaps, or something else?

(3) How do you balance seriousness and lightness in your life?

Prayer

God, thank You for helping us learn the balance between humor and seriousness—and the need for both.

(15)

Sophia Finds Communion with the Holy Spirit and People

"The seed, or grace of God, is small in its first appearance, even as the morning light; but as it is given heed to, and obeyed, it will increase in brightness, till it shines in the soul, like the sun in the firmament at its noon-day height."

—Elizabeth Bathurst (1655–1685)

Sophia attended a Methodist church. After she married a Quaker, she joined her husband in a so-called un-programmed Quaker Meeting. Unlike a Methodist Christian service, the un-programmed Quaker service was held in silence; there was no liturgy, music, pastor, sermon, formal blessings, and no communion, only meditative, prayerful silence.

Sophia observed that during the silence when a Quaker friend felt touched by the Holy Spirit he or she would stand up and speak briefly. They called this, "spoken ministry." She learned that the word "Quaker" expressed this spiritual experience of being called to give a message. The silence was intended to connect with the Holy Spirit.

The hour of Quaker worship calmed Sophia's rambling thoughts and she felt a connection with her inner Holy Spirit. Her soul felt God's presence. Occasionally spoken ministries often provided her with a kind of sermon that refreshed her spirit and quenched her spiritual thirst.

Still, the Quaker service remained strange to her. She missed the ritual practices of the Methodist liturgy in which she was raised. Off and on she continued to attend Methodist services.

At one point, Sophia decided to spend time away from the Quaker Meeting to explore different Methodist churches. She was looking to fill a gap in her spiritual needs that she couldn't fill at the Quaker Meeting. Perhaps she would find a church that would recapture her pre-Quaker spirituality?

In every church she visited, however, Sophia felt empty and lonely. She couldn't explain why; her search seemed to her to be a spiritual journey without roots. She was glad that her husband supported and was there to listen to her.

One Sunday morning, a year after she had last attended a Quaker Meeting, she felt a strong desire to return to the silent service. This time, an unusually deep silence fell upon her and questions arose: "Are you the body of Christ? Are you a part of this community?"

These questions helped her to examine her experiences while she explored different places of worship. She had a glimpse that her feelings of emptiness came from a sense of too little spiritual communion. She had taken wine and bread at Jesus' communion table, but she realized that for her, personal communion meant more. It meant experiencing a spiritual union in a community.

After the service that morning at the Quaker Meeting, she went to the fellowship hall. The familiar luncheon setting caught her attention: there were the usual tables, salad bowls, coffee mugs, several loaves of bread, and cookies. She recognized the monthly potluck, followed by a 2-hour meeting for business where the community dealt with organizational matters. Sophia knew that in most churches such business meetings were attended by staff, but in the Quaker Meeting, everyone could participate. It was considered a continuation of their worship and yet it wasn't easy for her to sit for such long business meetings.

On this day Sophia enjoyed the potluck luncheon together with other Quakers. She even volunteered to do the clean-up, and then joined the long meeting for business. It was a long day at the Meeting, but this time it was a joy for her, and she felt happy.

That evening she realized that the Holy Spirit had touched her in a special way; she felt she was part of a spiritual community that gave her meaningful quiet companionship and also a sense of belonging.

A few months later Sophia applied to be a member of the Quaker Meeting. A "clearness committee" was convened to discern her request for membership. Several questions were raised, and one member asked, "Why do you want to be an official Quaker member?" She replied, "I committed myself to follow the inner voice of the Holy Spirit that speaks to me. When Quakers sit together in worship, they commit to being led by this inner Holy Spirit. Of course, I don't mean to dismiss music or sermons or liturgy. They are very meaningful for many people."

Her new Quaker friends hosted a wonderful membership party to celebrate Sophia's faith and new membership. And she appreciated her husband who had waited for her while she journeyed through her own discernment to becoming a Quaker.

Spiritual Practice

(1) How have you experienced the presence of the Holy Spirit?

(2) How important for you is it to have a sense of spiritual community with others in your religious practice?

(3) Sit in a quiet place where your soul can rest and be tuned to the Spirit of God. What images, feelings, and thoughts come to you?

Prayer

Holy Spirit, help me to be in tune with you, to enjoy communal life with You, and with people in a faith community.

(16)

A Hurdle Becomes a Blessing

"For I, the Lord your God, hold your right hand; it is
I who say to you, 'Do not fear, I will help you.'"

—Isaiah 41:13

Jonathan was a bedside nurse. He worked three 12-hour shifts per week in a hospital unit where most of his patients were recovering from open-heart surgery. He enjoyed being with his patients very much and cherished the teamwork on the unit. He also studied towards achieving a master's degree in nursing with the goal of becoming a nurse practitioner. It was a challenge to manage school, internships, and work but the support from his wife and his faith community helped him greatly.

In the hospital, before he would enter a patient's room, he prayed for the strength and wisdom to provide the best care possible.

One day at work, Jonathan felt a sudden onset of chills, sore throat, and body aches. He groaned, "Oh no, this might be the flu." He was in the middle of the spring semester and was scheduled to work the next day as well—it was not a good time to get sick.

When his shift was over he rushed to Urgent Care. As he sat awaiting care, he became restless. The due date for his research paper was near and he still had a lot to write, and he began to wonder if he should postpone the class to the next semester. The doctor eventually diagnosed the flu and prescribed plenty of rest and water.

Back home, Jonathan was overwhelmed by the pressure of school and being sick. He couldn't work on the research paper and instead, laid miserably in bed. He felt as if he had to climb a very high mountain with no energy.

The next day Jonathan called in sick; his body aches were worse, and the pain medication didn't seem to help. He had now developed a fever and a persistent cough and returned to Urgent Care. This time the diagnosis was pneumonia... what a shock! The doctor gave him antibiotics and a note not to return to work for three weeks.

Over time the fever and cough diminished. It would still take several weeks before Jonathan completely regained his energy, but he was able to use the time off to finish and submit the research paper... what a relief that was!

A week passed before his grade was posted online: 99%! He thought to himself, "I can't believe it. The pneumonia was really a hidden blessing. I don't know if I could have finished that paper without the time off work that the illness gave me. Thank You, God, that You walked with me in this challenging time."

One year later, Jonathan had completed all courses and graduated with a Master of Science in Nursing degree.

He took the license examination and became a nurse practitioner.

Spiritual Practice

(1) Have you experienced a particular difficulty that turned out to be a blessing?

(2) How did you feel the presence of God during that time?

(3) What are the resources that you can access to overcome such a hurdle?

Prayer

God, help me to have an eye of faith to see that You uphold me in times of trouble.

(17)

Doris' Role as Mother Changed

"Young love is a flame—very pretty, often very hot and fierce, but still only light and flickering. The love of the older and disciplined heart is as coals, deep-burning, unquenchable."

—Henry Ward Beecher (1813–1887)

Doris had had five children. She raised them with strict discipline. She was not strong physically but was a moral role model for her children so that they would grow to become honest people. All her children except her youngest daughter, Suzanne, eventually married and moved into their own homes. Suzanne did have a daughter, Juli.

Suzanne and Juli continued to live with Doris. Suzanne had her own business and worked until the early evening while Juli was busy studying art in college.

Doris was 75 years old. She spent her days alone in her big apartment until Suzanne and Juli returned home.

Her beloved dog, who had been her daily companion, had passed on several years ago.

Doris had developed a daily routine at home: In the mornings she cooked meals for her daughter and granddaughter and watched educational and spiritual programs on TV, followed by house cleaning and laundry. Afterwards, she took a nap and in the evening she read three pages of the Bible as an ending of her day.

Doris began to develop pain in her hip. Medication helped some but over time the pain became worse and made it difficult for her to carry out her daily chores. Her daughter and granddaughter told her not to do anymore housework.

Their advice was not easy to accept for Doris; for more than 50 years Doris' world was focused on housework. The kitchen was the center of her life, and she didn't know what to do without her daily chores. Doris resisted the advice and continued her routine and, not surprisingly, her pain became worse. She was forced to end her work; no more cooking, cleaning, and doing laundry. She felt lost.

However, her pain brought on some positive changes among her children. Her oldest son, Tom, who lived nearby, visited her more often. Despite his busy schedule, he even prepared warm meals and picked her up to take her to doctor appointments. Tom would also pick up Suzanne so she could be home early and prepare evening meals. Doris watched her daughter cooking and was happy that she could teach her recipes.

Gradually Doris relaxed into her new life and began to have time for old memories. Her hip pain still bothered her, but she was thankful to God that all her children had grown up in good health and were settled in their lives. She began to observe them more carefully.

One evening Doris, Tom, and Suzanne sat at the dining room table enjoying tea. Doris told them, "In the beginning, I was very frustrated. I felt as if there was no place for me in this house." She paused and smiled, "Then I felt liberated. I didn't have to cook anymore! I had known that I needed to stop doing housework but I didn't know how to, even though my body couldn't handle it anymore." Doris was silent for a while. "You all are doing well. I feel relieved. Seeing you all grown and happy is all I need." She exhaled with a deep sigh.

Over time, Doris spent more time listening to her children and their issues. Listening helped Doris know how to pray for them. She also began to extend her prayers to include her church and social concerns.

Now as a "spiritual mother", Doris was still able to take care of her children and grandchildren.

Spiritual Practice

(1) Have you experienced change that resulted in a role change in your life?

(2) How did you adjust to the new role? What were the positive and challenging aspects during this transition?

(3) How do you nourish yourself and others in that new role?

Prayer

God, change can be so difficult. Sometimes I feel frustrated or fearful. Help me to adjust well during transitions in life so that I may nourish myself and others spiritually.

(18)

Tania Finds Her Calling and Reveals God as the Nurturer

"Joy is a net of love, by which you can catch souls."

—Mother Teresa (1910–1997)

Tania spent 12 years working at a small university. Even though she was satisfied with her teaching job and the financial stability it offered, she had gradually begun to feel fatigued and bored. Her commute was long, and she was often asked to perform repetitive administration tasks. However, she was hesitant to leave, it was not easy to take a risk and let go of financial stability.

She and her husband Jens prayed for discernment, asking Jesus, "Is this the right time to leave this job? Please, give me a sign."

Over time she became more and more uncomfortable with her work.

One afternoon, a student from her prayer group at the school came to her office. Cautiously he said to her that he felt that God might prepare her for a different job. Tania was surprised: "Why this, and why from one of her students?" She had never mentioned her discernment of her work with any of her students. Then, a few months later, another curious surprise: She received a call from a friend who had not contacted her for a long time. The friend asked her, "Are you struggling with leaving your present job?" Tania could no longer ignore the nudging of the Holy Spirit.

Tania and Jens took a year to prayerfully discern her next step. Finally, she was able to leave her teaching position and open her own small business.

In the beginning, her new role as a businesswoman was uncomfortable, but as time passed, she gradually adjusted to her new work. She joined a business networking group and met other business owners in various industries.

Tania enjoyed her new flexibility in scheduling her own time. As the owner, she arranged her workdays, sick days, and days off. The freedom she created with her business was an amazing gift. While her income fluctuated, she and her husband were still able to manage. Without the long commute, she found more time for relaxation. She remembered her love for cooking, playing guitar, reading books, and listening to sermons. Tania began to experience a whole new feeling of life.

Both Tania and her husband Jens had Thursdays off. Often, they began their day together by baking organic, multigrain bread from a simple recipe from their friend Douglas. Tania enjoyed baking bread very much.

On one particular Thursday off, however, Tania's hands were especially busy. She washed cucumbers, green and orange bell peppers, crunched garlic, and tossed it all into a wok, together with olive oil. She fried tofu for their lunch salad.

After lunch, Jens took a nap. Tania went on to slice ginger roots for tea. She thought this sunny day was perfect for drying sliced ginger out under the sun. She remembered how her grandmother would always dry vegetables during summer and fall to prepare for winter soups. She paused and smiled remembering her grandmother.

Cooking made Tania relaxed and gave her joy. This evening she planned to attend a women's prayer gathering. She made a tuna dip with lemon, pepper, chopped onion, and yogurt as a snack to bring. When Jens woke up from his nap and saw that his wife was still in the kitchen, he asked, "Why are you cooking so much?" She turned around and said, "Because I like it!"

In the evening Tania met her friends. They all enjoyed the tuna dip and fresh vegetables. Later that night, before going to sleep, she and her husband asked each other what God's grace was for them today. Tania shared how happy she felt cooking much of the day for her friends, for him, and for herself.

She said to Jens, "The joy of cooking was God's grace for me today. How nice that I now have the flexibility to schedule time for that!" Jens said, "Do you know the original meaning of the word used to describe God, El Shaddai'? It has been translated as 'Almighty,' but 'Shad' equally means 'The breasted one, the nurturer and strength-giver.'"

Tania said, "No wonder that I felt so happy when I cooked. I like to nurture people with food so that they can be strengthened." Jens continued, "Can you imagine how our individual lives and even the history of our world would have been different if we lived with an image of God as the breasted one, not as the Almighty? The world and our communities would be much more caring and nurturing."

Tania held what he said in her heart. It had not been easy to leave her secure teaching job, the financial stability that it provided, and to follow her inner leading to open her own business. Over time, however, she realized her joy came not from stability but from feeding souls. For her, cooking was one such channel to express a nurturing God.

Now Tania cooked not only for family and friends but also for poor people in her neighborhood. And although it wasn't always easy, she was glad she had changed her work situation.

Spiritual practice

(1) When do you feel joy in your everyday life?

(2) How do you express your joy?

(3) How do you experience God as a nurturer?

Prayer

God, thank You for joyfully nourishing us so that we ourselves can become nurturers for ourselves and others.

(19)

A Compassionate Presence

"God, who is everywhere, never leaves us. Yet God seems sometimes to be present, sometimes to be absent. If we do not know God well, we do not realize that God may be more present to us when God is absent than when God is present."

—Thomas Merton (1915–1968)

Elyse lived near the beautiful, warm ocean in Hawai'i. She worked as a chaplain in a local hospital. She enjoyed the peaceful nature of the islands and providing spiritual care to the hospital's ethnically diverse patients and their families. When she was a child, her mother was very ill. As a result, Elyse felt a calling for tending to the sick.

During her work, Elyse visited a 60-year-old Samoan woman in the oncology unit who was dying of cancer. The woman couldn't decide whether to return to Samoa to be with her family because the medical facilities there were not adequate for her needs, and yet she longed to spend the last stage of her life with her loved ones. Elyse listened to her struggle and accompanied her in this difficult decision-making process.

Elyse also liked to visit a Filipino woman in the hospice unit. She was a devout Catholic and, when she felt the time was right, she called all of her children together. For her last wish, she asked them simply to love one another. She told Elyse that she was ready to meet her beloved Lord Jesus Christ soon. "What a beautiful way to culminate her life," Elyse thought.

One evening it was Elyse's turn to be the on-call chaplain. She had dinner at the hospital cafeteria and rested, hoping that the night would be quiet and not too demanding.

At 10 p.m. she received a call from a social worker at the emergency department: A 19-year-old college student was admitted with a brain injury from a car accident. As Elyse entered the emergency room, the social worker asked her to wait for the patient's mother. When the mother arrived, she was very upset and feared her child would not survive. Elyse consoled her until she became calmer and slowly ready for any news she might soon receive.

Afterward, Elyse returned to her small chaplain room to sleep. It was almost midnight and before she fell asleep, she reflected on the people in her care, remembering another college girl who had a gunshot wound and miraculously had her speech restored. She prayed for the same healing for this young student.

Before she knew it, her beeper sounded again. It was half past 2 a.m. and a code had occurred in the cardiac surgery unit where a patient's heart had stopped beating. Elyse was a member of the code emergency team, and she stood outside the patient's room praying for the patient and the staff as the medical team attempted resuscitation.

After what seemed like an eternity the patient's heart began to beat again. Everyone sighed with relief and Elyse remarked to herself, "What intensive work this is."

It was now 3:30 a.m. and Elyse thought she should get some sleep, even if it was only for 30 minutes. Almost immediately after her head hit the pillow yet another pager alarm startled her awake. This time it came from the hospice unit. When Elyse arrived at the nursing station the night shift nurse briefly explained that an 80-year-old man had passed away two hours ago, and his wife had just arrived.

Elyse entered the patient's room to see the woman sitting beside her husband's bed. Elyse introduced herself and listened to the woman share stories about her husband. When Elyse tried to leave, the wife sighed, "I don't know how I can open my house when I return home. My husband always opened the door for me." With tears in her eyes, Elyse hugged her gently.

While she was still saying goodbye to the woman, Elyse received another call from the same hospice unit; another patient had just passed away. But this time there was no family and the night nurse asked, "Would you come over and bless the patient before his body is transferred to the morgue?"

Elyse entered the patient's room. There was no one there except her. She stood silently beside him and blessed him. Somehow, she felt God might have been with him when he took his last breath. She thought, "Who can accompany a person when they take their last breath except God?"

After this very long night of call, Elyse could no longer sleep. It was 7 a.m. and now time to prepare for visiting patients in the pre-operation unit. She washed her face and looked at herself in the mirror, breathing deeply. She then went and visited the patients who were awaiting surgery. Elyse felt their anxiety, comforted them, and held them in her prayers.

Finally, her "night" was over. Elyse reported to the incoming day shift chaplains what had happened and handed over her pager to the next on-call chaplain. Her supervisor said to her, "We appreciate your service, chaplain. This was an unusually hard night for you."

When Elyse left the hospital at 8 a.m. she sighed, "What a night indeed!" She was exhausted and filled with unprocessed emotions yet also knew she needed to relax. She swam in the pool at her apartment to unwind and then she went to bed and fell asleep instantaneously.

She woke up late in the afternoon, put on her shirt and pants and went down to the beach. A gorgeous sunset covered the sky in multiple shades of yellow, orange, and red. The palm trees swayed, and a soft breeze consoled her, giving her relief from the intensity of the previous night. She felt God soothing her by letting her experience nature and all its beauty. She felt God offering her compassion, just as God had offered it to her many patients.

Spiritual Practice

(1) How have you experienced a compassionate presence during a difficult time?

(2) Have you experienced the presence of God in an overwhelming situation?

(3) How did it make you feel when you offered compassion?

Prayer

God, thank You for offering us Your care, both visible and invisible.

(20)

What Really Matters

*"The harvest is plentiful, but the laborers are few;
therefore, ask the Lord of the harvest to send out
laborers into his harvest."*

—Luke 2:10

Josephine had a passion for praying with and for people. For her, prayer was a channel to healing her broken heart. Once during a prayer session, she felt the presence of Jesus as he seemed to ask her, "What do you want me to do for you?" Josephine replied, "Jesus, I want to heal people who are broken-hearted like me." At work in her health care clinic and while teaching, she provided both medical and emotional care for her patients.

Many years earlier, after she had married a German man, she wanted to perform Christian missionary work in Germany. Her husband Gerald, however, did not share that interest with her.

One day, Josephine met close friends with whom she had shared a prayer group with for many years. This couple had found their calling as missionaries to lepers in the African country of Burundi and they worked with the local people to build a hospital. They started Bible vacation school programs for children and had made every effort to adjust to life in Burundi, working with the locals, and eating local foods. Their stories challenged Josephine who felt that something in her life was missing. She thought that her passion for mission work in Germany had never come to life.

After her reflection, she made a decision. "Gerald," she said, "I want to visit Germany and spend a week in a monastery. I want to discern what God wants me to do there. Perhaps there is a need for my gift in providing pastoral care to their broken-hearted."

Gerald had heard her desire to do mission work in Germany many times before, but he noticed that this time was different; Josephine was determined to go. He suggested that they pray together for several weeks. Perhaps there was a way, after all, for her to support people who had not reconciled the emotional pains of their pasts.

After a month of prayer, Gerald said, "Josephine, I like your idea to visit Germany. I am thinking that rather than staying in a monastery over there, why don't you start your mission work in my family? You could visit my mother, Heidi. She is having great pain as she recovers from knee surgery. My mother's partner, Frank, also has severe pain in his lower back. You could even offer acupuncture treatment to ease their pains."

Gerald also spoke about his mother's emotional needs and how she still greatly missed her father who had died in

World War II. And Frank had just recently lost his daughter to cancer. "A visit to this older couple is truly mission work that uses your gifts," he added, and Josephine agreed.

The following Sunday, Josephine and Gerald joined in a worship service. The sermon seemed to be directly addressing Josephine as the pastor proclaimed, "One leader does grandiose work in doing ministry; another is doing small work quietly without being noticed."

Towards the end of the service, there was an opportunity to receive personal prayer in the chapel corner of the big church. Gerald took Josephine's hand and led her there. A tall African American woman, Veronica, opened her arms for them. Gerald told her, "My wife will visit my mother and her partner in Germany next week, all alone. It will be her first time there by herself." His voice trembled and he had tears in his eyes. The woman placed her strong hands gently on their shoulders and prayed for them. Josephine felt her husband's deep caring and support for her mission trip.

On the plane en route to Hamburg, Josephine felt strange without her husband, but she was also very excited about what God would do with her once she arrived.

For seven days Josephine spent time with Heidi and Frank, including sharing every meal together. Josephine thought to herself, "I never had such an intimate time with my own parents." She felt as if she was having communion with Heidi and Frank. She accompanied Heidi when she went to see different doctors and provided acupuncture treatments for Heidi's knee pain and Frank's lower back.

One day while they were driving on a country road Heidi wanted to stop to take a short walk on a nearby trail. She explained to Josephine, "This is where many Jews were forced to walk to concentration camps. Many couldn't make it and they died here." Heidi was solemn. Josephine tried to imagine the suffering of the people on the marches; she prayed in silence, asking God for forgiveness.

Heidi shared many stories about her family, in particular when her father had been killed in World War II. She was a young girl at the time and yet now, almost 80 years old, she still missed her father. She organized letters that he had sent to her mother during the war and reread them more than once. Josephine listened to Heidi's unresolved grief. Frank usually didn't share much about his feelings, but he, too, began to open his heart and share his deep sorrow over his losses. Both his wife and his daughter had died of cancer. Josephine understood Frank and his quiet ways better now. She thought to herself, "How could he ever bear such deep pain?" As she listened to their grief, Josephine silently prayed, "Jesus, please console their hearts."

During her visit, Josephine also worked on writing an article. Heidi read her draft and gave her feedback and Frank corrected her English grammar. They enjoyed these simple moments sharing and laughing together.

One day, Josephine joined one of Heidi and Franks' neighborhood gatherings. She listened to the villagers' stories as Frank translated the German into English, and Josephine was grateful for Frank's consideration. Most neighbors grew up in communist East Germany and shared their difficulties of having faith in God. The government strongly discouraged any belief other than in the state. As she was listening to their struggles, Josephine felt as if she had taken a time machine back to East Germany. She silently prayed for the neighbors so that God might heal their hearts.

Josephine also attended a small Protestant church service during her visit. She was happy to meet one of Heidi's friends who had also grown up in East Germany. Josephine was surprised to see the friend sing church hymns. Frank also sang and she was delighted to find he had a beautiful voice.

In the afternoons Josephine had time for herself and would walk around the neighborhood. She saw the beauty of each house and silently blessed those living in them with the name of Jesus.

One evening as it neared her time to return to the U.S., Josephine came to her room and thought to herself, "Here I am, well fed, enjoying cake and tea every day, and sleeping in a cozy room." She remembered her missionary friends in Burundi who lived among poor people. She, in contrast, felt as if she was in a comfortable retreat center. She prayed, "God, is this the mission work that you wanted me to do in Germany? I don't know what else to do." She heard a small voice within her, saying, "Josephine, what do you think mission work is? It is to care and love people deeply with the love that you receive from me." Josephine felt tears rising in her eyes.

She indeed had cared for and consoled this elderly couple. She asked God for forgiveness for Germany's horrific past, and she blessed the couple's neighbors. Josephine felt that God had brought her to Germany for this purpose and she realized God wanted her to learn how much God cares for and loves all people.

Finally, Josephine returned home. Gerald welcomed her with a big hug, "My beloved German missionary has come back!"

Josephine had experienced God's love and put it in motion. She continued to pray for people in Germany—with God's continued love.

Spiritual Practice

(1) What special gift of yours would you like to share with others?

(2) What is your unique way of using the gift of serving people?

(3) How did experiencing God's love transform your life and the lives of others you might know?

Prayer

God, help us to find our special gifts. Guide us in letting love infuse our daily work, so that we may embody Your heart.

(21)

Dietrich Experiences His Passion in a New Way

"Be kind to one another, tenderhearted, forgiving one another, as God, in Christ forgave you."

—Ephesians 4:32

Dietrich, a pastor, had a great passion to guide people to Biblical sites in Israel and Palestine. He wanted to refresh and ground anew their Christian faith and had dedicated much of his life to his work.

Now that his children had grown up and had their own families, however, he wished he had spent more time with them.

One day Dietrich received an email from his oldest son Joachim. Joachim had made new friends who were active in fostering peace and understanding between Jewish Israelis and Palestinians. His wife Sue suggested that they take a trip there with his dad since his dad knew the land so well. They asked Dietrich if he wanted to visit the Holy

Land with them and within ten minutes, Dietrich emailed back, "Yes."

Dietrich looked very much forward to this trip. He thought that it would be a great opportunity to get to know his oldest son better.

The three arranged to meet at the airport in Tel Aviv. When Dietrich arrived, Joachim and Sue waved a small Israeli flag. His son hugged him and said, "Welcome, Dad, to Tel Aviv!"

Their first stop was the ancient port city of Jaffa. Parts of the city were in a festive mood in preparation for Sukkot, an important Jewish holiday that commemorates the sheltering of the Israelites in the wilderness. In Jaffa, Jewish and Palestinian young people mingled and talked, smoked, and drank together. Dietrich thought to himself, "What a different world it is here! There is no conflict like in Jerusalem or Hebron." He felt very refreshed as he cherished this moment late in the night in the warm Mediterranean summer air, enjoying a beer and great conversation outdoors with his son and daughter-in-law.

The next morning, they explored the city. They tasted local food and rested at a corner in front of the house of Simon the Tanner. Here, according to the New Testament, Peter received a revelation from God. Dietrich saw how Joachim and Sue sat in prayer. He thought to himself, "What a pious young couple they are."

On the way from Jaffa to Galilee, Dietrich visited the Jewish family of a dear friend with whom he had done reconciliation work for many years. His friend had passed away, but Dietrich continued to keep in touch with his family. He and Joachim wore a Kippah, the Jewish head covering for men. They all enjoyed a lengthy dinner together and talked about the reconciliation work that Dietrich and his friend did. Dietrich was happy that he could share with Joachim and Sue what was so dear to his heart.

It was a delightful journey to Lake Galilee and then to Nazareth. The lake was calm and quiet with a gentle breeze and Dietrich and Joachim woke up early in the morning to take a swim.

At the breakfast table, Sue asked: "How was Lake Galilee?" Joachim replied, "When I saw the beautiful sun rising over the Golan Heights across the lake, I felt as if Jesus was rising today and every morning again and again!" Sue observed what an incredible and Divine gift Joachim's insight was for them.

They stayed at Lake Galilee for several days. Dietrich guided them to an archeological site of an ancient synagogue, to the place of the miracle of Jesus feeding the 5,000, and to Capernaum where Jesus is believed to have performed many healings.

They were sad to leave this beautiful land of Galilee, but time called them to travel onward to Nazareth, and then along the Jordan River past Jericho up through the desert hills to Jerusalem. There, at the Western Wall, Dietrich inserted a prayer note into a small crack in between the building stones. He prayed, "Lord, please bring peace in Israel and Palestine."

Many tourists were at the Church of the Holy Sepulcher, the church that stands over what is believed to be the site of Jesus' crucifixion and empty tomb. On the Via Dolorosa,

a man carried a cross followed by a small crowd of wor-
shippers. Dietrich didn't care much for this kind of com-
memoration, noting that Jesus most likely didn't carry
his cross on this particular street but more likely further
south. He explained that he wanted his tour participants
to grow their faith independent of historical reports which
were not always accurate.

Afterwards, Dietrich took Sue and Joachim to the Yad
Vashem Holocaust memorial. For Dietrich, this unforgettable terror was not only a horror committed by a state.
It also impacted his life personally as a Christian and as a
German citizen. He saw his son kneeling down in silence in
the Hall of Remembrance where each concentration camp
was listed. He felt the deep, heavy memory of the past
lying on their shoulders.

For the last two days of their tour, Dietrich chose to
visit Bethlehem, the birthplace of Jesus. They met with his
friend Wafa, a Palestinian tour guide who had grown up in
Germany. She shared her pain over her sons' daily struggles at checkpoints on their way to work. Wafa took them
to her family's olive garden that was now divided by the
barrier wall that surrounded a settlement.

Hearing the stories of local people and feeling the
depth of their pain made their visit incredibly special.

Afterwards, they drove south through the dry land-
scape to the city of Hebron and Abraham's tomb. They
soon found themselves in the middle of an intersection
with Palestinian protestors on one side and the Israeli
army on the other. They heard shots and the locals advised
them to leave quickly. As they made their way away from

the protest, they stopped at a pottery store. Sue wanted to have a memory of their trip and purchased mugs and plates. Joachim said, "Our kitchen will shine with colorful Palestinian pottery." Wafa smiled and replied, "Please don't forget us after you return home."

Their final visit in the West Bank was the educational farm Tent of Nations. People from around the world came here to learn about local farming and non-violence. Joachim was deeply impressed by the sign on the entrance. "We refuse to be enemies" it read, and he felt the truth of it ring deeply.

Back in Israel, they spent a night at a village called Neve Shalom/Wahat al Salam. There, Jewish and Palestinian families lived, worked, and raised their children together. The three of them contemplated: "Surely, there was a path to peace when there was such deep commitment."

On the last evening, they sat on a bench together, reflecting on the last ten days of their visits to Israel and Palestine. Dietrich said, "This trip was so relaxing for me. I had none of the obligations and responsibilities that I usually have as a guide for a group of 40 people. I sometimes had such deep, Divine experiences on those trips but there was so little opportunity to share them. I am glad that I could share these meaningful moments with you two." They fell into a companionable silence for a while and watched the sun go down.

Joachim then spoke in reply, "Dad, we got to know what is so important to you on this trip. I am glad to have had this time with you and to get to know you better. And with your guidance and explanations about the historical sites, the trip also helped us to understand the Bible better. I feel that my faith in Jesus is growing deeper in the spirit behind the stories."

Dietrich was very happy that his son and daughter-in-law not only had joined him on this journey, but also joined in his passion.

Spiritual Practice

(1) How have you developed your passion?

(2) How can you share it with others?

(3) Have you had the experience of participating in other people's passions? How did it help your own spiritual growth, even healing?

Prayer

God, thank You for Your passion to reach out to people and to help us to develop that passion in our hearts.

(22)

Martin Realizes What Carries Him

"Restore to me the joy of your salvation, and sustain in me a willing spirit."

—Psalm 51:12

Martin, a Caucasian college student, grew up in Africa as the child of missionaries. His parents were devoted Christians and had moved to Africa to serve local farmers by working together with them to develop an irrigation system.

Martin was a sensitive child. His parents had been supportive, but it was deeply challenging for him to be exposed to poverty and unfamiliar cultures. Making new friends had been hard as his family frequently moved from one place to the next, from one mission project to the next.

He felt safe in the Christian faith community and enjoyed a close relationship with God. He spent much of his time in church and his love for music and guitar was also a solace to him.

When Martin was an adolescent, he went through a psychological crisis. He needed hospitalization and was isolated from his beloved church, his friends, and also his family. Since then he was afraid to be too close to God.

At age 19, Martin moved to America by himself to pursue a college degree. The first year was tough as he struggled to meet academic demands and dealt with loneliness. It was also quite a cultural shock, having grown up around poverty and now finding himself living with fellow students that had smartphones and fancy cars. Everything was fast-moving; the abundance he experienced throughout the campus overwhelmed him since he himself had very little.

Still, Martin felt grateful to be able to study at a university. During summer vacation he visited his uncle and aunt in Los Angeles. They cared for him deeply, listened to his struggles, and talked with him about his future direction.

One evening, his aunt asked Martin whether he wanted to explore his concerns through spiritual direction. At the university, Martin was part of a Christian community. Something, however, was missing. He yearned to be emotionally close to God but at the same time, he feared it because of his past psychosis.

Martin contacted the spiritual director whom his aunt had recommended.

Sandra, the spiritual director, was very attentive to his story. She asked him whether he would like to reflect on his spiritual journey. She gave him a sheet of paper and showed him how to draw a spiritual map. It included special occasions, traumas, ups and downs, and mishaps.

As Martin wrote and drew on the paper, he was surprised that he marked as the starting point of his spiritual journey the time of his hospitalization. Sandra asked, "How was your experience of God in those days?" An image arose in his mind and he saw himself in the middle of a wildfire that threatened to consume him.

He said to Sandra, "I think my relationship with God was like a burning wildfire, consuming me. I was too enmeshed in it. I was in the fire, but there was no me. Only God."

He continued the exercise and began to draw parts of his college life. He felt this was a new, second stage of his spiritual journey and he found that he had opened up more to others. Although he liked to study by himself, he did not want to be confined to an isolated dorm room. Instead, he went to the library where he was surrounded by other students. He felt their presence encouraged him to focus on studying.

Sandra asked him how his image of God had changed during college. He answered her, "God is like a big tree to me now. Around this tall, strong tree there are many small trees. I am one of those small trees, having a little distance from the big tree, but still under its shade being nurtured and protected. My small tree is growing independently yet maintains a close relationship with the big tree." He felt as if all these small trees could be people, growing spiritually in connection with God.

With such self-reflection, Martin slowly began to feel safe and close to God again. God no longer overwhelmed and consumed him like a wildfire. He realized that he had a healthy distance from God now, and was no longer en-meshed, but still and ever more under God's nurturing protection.

And he discovered how music had carried him over the years. He said, "Now I can pick up my guitar again to sing and praise God."

Spiritual Practice

(1) What was your image of God when you were in a time of crisis?

(2) How has your image of God and your relationship with God changed over time?

(3) What has continuously upheld you on your spiritual journey?

Prayer

God, help me to see the spiritual thread that has sustained me through the ups and downs in my life.

(23)

A Humble Blessing

"Out of the believer's heart shall flow rivers of living water."

—John 7:38b

Jerome was studying systematic theology in a Ph.D. program in Frankfurt, Germany. He was a bright scholar and had a big pastoral heart; he cared for people's souls. He grew up as the son of a preacher in the American South.

His vision was to someday become a president of an American university.

In Frankfurt, Jerome met Fabian who was in town for a summer job. Fabian enjoyed being involved in the university's campus ministry when he was a student and had himself taken several classes in theology. Both men were in their late thirties. They stayed in the same seminary dormitory since it was inexpensive and offered a quiet, spiritual atmosphere.

They became good friends; Jerome was happy to make a German friend and practice the language and they both liked to talk about theologians like John Cobb, Paul Tillich, and Friedrich David Schleiermacher.

They also enjoyed having tea together. One evening, after Fabian had finished his work, he visited Jerome. Jerome asked Fabian to give him a few minutes and he walked to the kitchen. Fabian thought that Jerome might bring some tea, but it seemed to be taking him a little longer than usual.

When Jerome returned, Fabian saw a big green bucket in his hands, rather than mugs and a teapot, Fabian was curious about what Jerome was doing when he asked him to wait just a few more minutes.

This time when Jerome returned, he was carrying a towel and soap. Jerome poured some of the liquid soap into the bucket of water. He said to his friend, "Fabian, I will wash your feet. Don't worry. Give me your feet." Fabian was calm as he allowed his friend to wash his feet.

Fabian felt several emotions while his friend washed his feet: warmth, acceptance, and love. He didn't ask Jerome why he was doing this; he remembered a time with his girlfriend Sue when he did the same thing. He had washed her feet in the solemn way that Jesus had washed his disciples' feet. Jesus asked his disciples to serve others as he served them, and he recalled that it was a humble and meaningful experience for them both. It was a way of practicing mutual respect and acceptance before each other and before God. He was grateful that Jerome reminded him of an important time spent with his girlfriend.

Fabian was also grateful that their friendship transcended history and societal patterns as Jerome was black and he was white. He thought to himself that someday Jerome would indeed become a great scholar because he had such a caring heart.

Later that evening Fabian couldn't wait to phone Sue and share his experience earlier with Jerome. "Sue," he said, "I purposely tried not to think about why Jerome was washing my feet; I just appreciated it for what it was. I did not analyze it. I simply cherished this moment of mutual humbleness and dignity."

A couple of years later, Jerome returned to America to become a professor for systematic theology at a college, teaching students and serving them as a university chaplain. Despite the distance, their friendship continued.

Jerome often thought about Fabian when he reflected on his own faith. He remembered Fabian's warm and gentle personality and knew that both he and Sue were involved in spiritual care. Likewise, Fabian often remembered that Jerome had been a role model for them in the way Jerome combined scholarship with a caring heart.

On the day of Jerome's inauguration ceremony as professor, he received a call from Fabian, "Jerome, congratulations! You are now a professor. Many blessings my friend! May you become university president in the near future." They laughed together.

Jerome and Fabian both cherished their friendship as they respected and encouraged each other to be who they were.

Spiritual Practice

(1) Have you ever experienced the gift of being served with a humble and unexpected blessing?

(2) How did you respond to that gift?

(3) What hinders or encourages you to appreciate mutual acceptance in your life?

Prayer

Jesus, help me to learn mutual respect and appreciation and may it flow freely from my heart.

(24)

How Can I Find Something That is Very Dear to Me Again?

"Or what woman having ten silver coins, if she loses one of them, does not light a lamp, sweep the house, and search carefully until she finds it?"

—Luke 15:8

Steven liked to study at the beach. It was his favorite place. He enjoyed walking along the shore, resting and praying there. A small, shell-shaped beach tent was his personal retreat center.

He would see other beachgoers laughing, carrying surfboards, and riding bicycles. It was like a summer painting in front of his eyes.

One day he discovered an Italian restaurant nearby that would fit his student budget. He loved the restaurant's open outdoor atmosphere. He ordered what would become his favorite dish, a steaming hot plate of vegetable spaghetti with a delicious sauce.

When Steven returned home that evening, however, he realized that he had left his bag behind at the restaurant. And in the bag were his notes from a class he was taking on psycho-social primary care. He cherished this class and kept meticulous notes; he couldn't bear to think he had lost them.

Steven returned to the restaurant the next afternoon and politely asked a waitress whether a black bag had been found. She looked around cursorily, returned, and said, "No, sorry." She was a little bit dismissive and Steven was frustrated by her indifference. He tried to figure out ways to find his notebook, knowing that he had left his bag on a chair there just the day before. Yet instead of bugging the waitress, he went back to the beach and prayed about what to do.

When he arrived at the beach, he was still upset and disappointed by the waitress's attitude. He decided to enter into silent prayerful listening. It came to him that it was better not to be upset and instead return to the restaurant later that day for an early dinner. In the meantime, he studied.

When it was time to eat, he sat at the same table and ordered the same hot vegetable spaghetti dish. He hoped someone might remember him and his bag.

The same waitress served him. This time she was polite but when he asked whether she saw his bag, she once again made little to no attempt to find it.

Then Steven saw the manager standing nearby and talking with the waitress. He approached him and asked about his bag. The manager was not very friendly, but he made an effort and called his colleague who did remark that he *had seen* a black bag on his desk the previous night.

Low and behold, the bag was found and returned to Steven. Alas, it was empty! His cherished notebook was not in it!

The manager asked another waiter to look in the trash. Steven and the waiter worked together to open several bags filled with leftover food and empty cans. It was not fun, but there it was! Wet, though thankfully spared of any tomato sauce stains. He could still read his notes. Steven was incredibly grateful and said to himself in quiet thanksgiving, "Thank you, God, manager, and waiter!"

He took the notebook back to the beach. While he rested under his sunshade, the warm summer wind flipped the pages of his notebook, drying them one by one. Steven observed with a big smile. His time spent in prayer, he felt, had guided him well.

Spiritual Practice

(1) What have you cherished in your life and then lost?

(2) How could you go about finding your lost treasure?

(3) Might you be able to replace it in a different way altogether?

Prayer

God, help me to find my treasure. It is lost in the midst of my busy life.

(25)

The Inherent Dignity of Everyone

"Walk cheerfully on the earth, answering that of God in everyone."

—George Fox (1624–1691)

Camilla ran her own retail business. Every Wednesday morning, she joined a meeting with other business owners, including a dentist, a chiropractor, an accountant, and a realtor. The meeting was a mutual referral network.

Recently, Camilla experienced severe lower back pain. To counter it, she was determined to walk for one hour every day. Similar to her early morning prayer, walking became a daily ritual.

After the networking meeting was over, she walked to her store. On the way she noticed more and more homeless people sleeping on sidewalks, church lawns, or at various corners of buildings.

This particular time she saw a homeless man lying on a sidewalk, but unlike other homeless people, he had no belongings with him. He wore a shabby shirt and jeans and held a broken pole in his right hand. Though exhausted, his face looked rather peaceful, and it seemed as if nothing mattered to him.

Camilla looked at him from a distance. As she came closer, she could not just pass by him. She saw no body movement and she feared he might have fainted. Several times she walked by him, back and forth. Finally, she found the courage to address him, "Hello, hello!"

There was no response. She took a five-dollar bill out of her purse to give to him. She said to him, "I want to give you some money."

The motionless man opened his eyes and looked at her. She was relieved. She handed the money to him, and he sat up and put it in his pocket. He replied to her, "Thank you, Madam," and laid back down.

Camilla continued to walk toward her store. She thought, "How can I help a person like him? I gave him a little money but what can my little bit do for him, given the enormity of his helplessness and deprivation?"

Later that day she received a call from a customer who apologized for not having paid his expenses on time. He asked whether he could deliver a check in the afternoon.

Camilla answered him, "Yes, of course. Thank you for remembering. I know we all get busy."

The customer came and when he paid, he added an extra five dollars. "Please, Camilla, keep the extra money. I know it is not easy to own a small business and I am sorry I was late."

The money she had given away earlier in the day had just returned to her.

After the customer left, Camilla thought that she should not make too much of this coincidence though she did feel something special had happened. It was as if God recognized her concern for the homeless man.

Her day was brightened, and she was happy. She felt the presence of God amid her work. She was encouraged. Somehow the homeless man gave Camilla a much bigger gift than she had given him.

She thought to herself, "What I can do may not be much, but it is something." She began to support a breakfast service for local homeless women and would sometimes buy an extra lunch when she knew that there was going to be a homeless person on her way from a restaurant.

She made a special effort to recognize each homeless person she came upon and prayed for each one she met.

Spiritual Practice

(1) Can you remember a time when you experienced the presence of God in an unlikely setting, situation, or person?

(2) What is your particular spiritual base from which you reach out to those who are in difficult situations?

(3) What enables you to see human dignity when you see people who are in desperate situations?

Prayer

God, help us to respect the inherent dignity of human beings.

(26)

Abundant Life

"In the morning sow your seed, and at evening do not let your hands be idle; for you do not know which will prosper, this or that, or whether both alike will be good."

—Ecclesiastes 11:6

Maria and Toni moved to an apartment in the rear part of a small duplex. The apartment in the front was rented to a musician, Sarah. An Indian family also shared the property in a separate house across a narrow driveway which all the tenants shared.

Maria and Toni enjoyed the large backyard that opened up behind their home. It was several times bigger than their apartment and offered them a wonderful view of palm trees and the wide-open sky. There was a small shack in the corner of the yard where a neighbor occasionally lowered one of the walls like a door and set up a charming carpentry shop.

The property was quiet, and the tenants felt as if they lived in a small retreat center. When Maria and Toni woke up in the morning, stray cats would be resting on the roofs of their cars.

Maria wanted to create space for a vegetable garden and to plant more fruit trees. The previous resident had planted a lemon and an orange tree and roses blossomed beautifully in two large pots.

One Saturday morning, Maria and Toni woke up early and started to make the vegetable garden area. They dug soil, poured organic fertilizers, and watered the space until the soil was thoroughly wet. By the afternoon four areas were prepared. Voilà!

Toni was happy that he was able to help his wife with this project. She was alone at home for many weekends because he had to work every other weekend and it was not easy for them to have enough quality time together.

A few days later, Toni told Maria that he had given one vegetable area to the lady in the front house and another area to the Indian family. That left only two areas for Maria to plant. She was a little disappointed, but she said, "Let's plant seeds in our garden, Toni." Their hands became busy with sowing organic seeds for tomatoes, beans, arugula, lettuce, carrots, and cucumbers.

During summer evenings Maria watered all four vegetable gardens, and in time she found her neighbors watered hers as well. The neighbors' gardens were full of cherry tomatoes, and a mint bush grew well under the shade of the leaves of green bean plants. Arugula and lettuce flourished in Maria's garden, and she shared them with her neighbors. Their garden had become a true community garden.

Maria started the habit of tossing all of the seeds she came across into the garden. After she ate honeydew, she threw its seeds in an open patch of the garden. Soon she saw a small honeydew fruit growing. Then she planted pumpkin seeds, and a small pumpkin grew.

She was overjoyed. Wherever she planted seeds, life grew.

Birds often sang from the neighbors' trees. They dropped sunflower seeds near their robust vegetable patches. Within no time, strong stems shot up and bright yellow sunflowers lightened the yard.

Maria realized with gratitude the gift of the abundant life she had been given in the creation and sharing of her garden.

Spiritual Practice

(1) How do you plant or cultivate the joy of life?

(2) Can you think of a plan, including when and where?

(3) How can you share your unique joy with others?

Prayer

Source of Life, we thank You for opening our eyes to see the hidden power of life. Help us to participate in cultivating it within ourselves and with others.

(27)

How Martha's Sadness Over Not Conceiving Her Own Child Led Her to Herself

"As a deer longs for flowing streams, so my soul longs for you, O God. My soul thirsts for God, for the living God. When shall I come and behold the face of God? My tears have been my food day and night. [...] Why are you cast down, O my soul, and why you disquieted within me? Hope in God; for I shall again praise God, my help and my God."

—Psalm 42:1–3a, 5

Martha wished to have a child even though she and her husband Jerry married late. They were already in their early forties and hoped to have a baby soon; the couple prayed to God to grant them their wish.

Martha often wondered what the child might look like. On their wedding night, Jerry had dreamt of a 3-year-old boy, very healthy and playing cheerfully. Now Martha remembered how happy that dream had made them back then.

But life didn't go the way they had hoped and prayed. Martha and Jerry had to face one negative pregnancy test after the other.

They decided to visit a highly recommended fertility doctor at a large university medical center. They underwent many exams—hormone blood tests, sperm count, tubular patency. Due to her age, the doctor warned them that if they did conceive their child might have birth defects.

Martha and her husband decided to pursue an intra-uterine injection. But the pregnancy test came out negative as well. Sad feelings swept over them. The medical procedure and the several months of preparation left Martha emotionally and physically exhausted.

The couple sought help in dealing with their overwhelming disappointment by joining an infertility support group. Participants came from many different ethnic backgrounds. Martha and Jerry enjoyed the group very much.

During the first meeting, Martha heard the other couples' deep despair, feelings of guilt, and blame. One woman went through recurrent miscarriages; another woman had a stillborn baby and continued to grieve over the loss; one couple went as far as selling their house to cover the cost of several in vitro fertilizations.

Martha was shocked by their stories. They were both painful and heartbreaking.

After that first meeting of the support group, Martha had a strange feeling of appreciation surging up from deep inside her. She told Jerry that she felt her own emotional pain couldn't compare to the sorrow of the other couples. Ironically, their stories had reduced her own feelings of sadness.

The couples she met and the stories she heard made Martha examine her own desire to have a baby; soul searching not out of desperation but out of a sense of peace. Martha often heard that a child was a necessity to strengthen a marriage and she asked herself if that cultural belief suited her. She agreed that a child could provide stability, but a series of additional questions arose in her mind: "Why is it that I want a child?", "What if I don't have my own biological one?", "Should we adopt?", and "Will our marriage lack the particular bonding that having a child can add?"

As she held these thoughts in her heart, she also noted how much she appreciated her husband's presence. She was very grateful for that feeling.

Another question arose around why her wish for a child was apparently not as desperate as those of the other couples in the group. The questions challenged her to face honestly who she really was and what she really wanted.

Amid her self-examination and prayer, she was led to more fundamental questions, such as "Who am I?", "Will I still be worthy if I don't have my own biological child?", "Will I still be enough?", and "Where can I find that intimate love that I may have with my own child?"

As she reflected, Martha became aware that it was her relationship with God which was opening her heart and mind to think differently. She began to see herself not as *what she had*, but as *who she was* in God.

Her new understanding and acceptance of herself extended into greater compassion and loving feelings toward others.

Spiritual Practice

(1) What hinders you from accepting yourself socially, relationally, or spiritually?

(2) What do you cherish most in your relationships with yourself, your spouse, or your family?

(3) How might you be able to reconcile with God's help and a new spiritual understanding a heart's desire, a challenge in your life or in helping someone else with their struggles?

Prayer

God, help me to create light and hope together with You so that I may understand and accept myself and others.

(28)

Marlon Restores Her Strength

"If any of you is lacking in wisdom, ask God, who gives to all generously and ungrudgingly, and it will be given you."

—James 1:5

Marlon was lively, sociable, and spiritual. She worked for a school community, cared for children, and listened to the parents' concerns.

Recently, however, she began to withdraw from making contact with parents and from her beloved faith community. She preferred to be alone, read inspirational books, and share occasional phone calls with her siblings. She also engaged in her own art and whenever she thought of it, she felt her spirit's lift.

Marlon had two concerns: her own withdrawal from people and her husband Jorgen who suffered from severe depression. It both saddened her and made her nervous.

Lately, Jorgen had also been emotionally withdrawing from her and that added to her own anxiety.

Marlon visited her friend Dana whom she talked with often. "Dana," she said with tears in her eyes, "I am scared and depressed whenever I feel as if Jorgen is leaving me emotionally."

Dana listened to her and said, "Marlon, why don't we pray in silence and see what insights God may grant us?" Quietly, Marlon laid out her concerns in front of God, asking for help, insights and wisdom, "God, here are my concerns. Help me to deal with them. What do you want me to do? What do you want me to learn? Give me the wisdom to handle my concerns."

The two friends listened to God silently. After some time, Dana spoke and said that in the quiet a feeling came to her as if a big rock was on Marlon's life path. Without hesitation, Marlon said, "That is how I feel! I am stuck. I don't know how to remove this heavy rock."

Dana knew that Marlon liked to express herself by drawing. Dana gave Marlon a piece of paper, crayons, and pencils. She said, "Marlon, would you like to draw how you feel?"

Marlon sketched a road with a big rock in the center that she colored black. She then added three small flowers onto the rock with a yellow crayon and added drizzling rain and clouds in gray with a colorful small rainbow.

Marlon looked at the piece of paper in front of her and then added a person standing between the rock and its surroundings. The person was pointing to the rock. Marlon then drew books, a phone, several big trees, and two small hands in prayer behind the figure.

Dana asked about the meaning of her drawing and Marlon explained the objects one by one.

"The small flowers are my children; the drizzling rain is my sadness; the rainbow, inspirational books, phone, and prayer hands are my nurturers that feed my withered soul."

Dana then asked Marlon what the figure was doing. She suggested that it seemed to be a channel receiving light and energy from the nurturing items and then passing it on to the rock.

Marlon was a little surprised and replied, "Really? I didn't realize that I was the channel giving light and energy to the rock. I can give more light and energy!" With a yellow crayon, she scribbled rays of light and filled all the empty space on the rock.

Marlon continued, "I always thought the rock should be removed. But perhaps the rock should not be removed after all." She smiled, "I can't change my husband's depression. Instead, I can focus on my art that sustains me and may serve to inspire Jorgen to find a healing path of his own. The art also ignites the light of God within me and enables me to absorb an enormous amount of Divine energy."

She took a deep breath. She was silent for a while and then she said softly, "I have been wanting to be a successful artist, but my personal suffering and spiritual practice has led me to a different, more profound goal. I want to be an artist who manifests the Divine and spiritual inspiration in my work. I can now see my own transformation."

A few months later, Marlon received a scholarship dedicated to artists who incorporated spirituality into their art. Her work blossomed and she had many shows on her own and together with other artists. In time, her husband and his psychiatrist found the right dosage for his medication. It also helped them a lot that his employer was very supportive.

Marlon felt Jorgen gradually open up more to her. He shared his feelings with her honestly when he was going through intense anxiety. She made him a calming tea, listened to him, and provided support with her greater understanding.

Marlon and Jorgen were glad they had each other during these trying times. Her deeper relationship with God continued to help her to ride life's occasional ups and downs—together.

Spiritual Practice

(1) Can you imagine or draw a picture of your present emotional and spiritual life?

(2) If you have your own "big rock," what might it be and where is it positioned in the picture?

(3) How do you want to handle that rock?

(4) What are your emotional and spiritual resources?

Prayer

God, grant us Your wisdom to recognize all the resources You have given us to handle our anxieties and concerns.

(29)

Caroline Discerns How to Prioritize Her Work

"Do you not know that you are God's temple and that God's spirit dwells in you?"

—1 Corinthians 3:16

Caroline worked as a professional counselor. For as long as she could remember she had nurtured a desire to write a book. Because of her busy schedule, however, she kept postponing her writing. She had operated a small counseling center together with other psychotherapists for more than five years now, and even though there were occasional challenges the center had steadily stabilized as she received more and more referrals over the years.

Caroline generally had a regular stream of clients on Fridays, but then, for two Fridays in a row, all her clients canceled their appointments. It felt odd and more than coincidental. When she shared her concern with her husband, he shrugged it off. "It can happen," he replied. Still,

Caroline didn't dismiss the question of why this had happened now. Never in the past five years did she have so many cancellations in such a short time.

Caroline also realized that she was experiencing a strange feeling of emptiness during her busier days. She began to wonder if the counseling work was really enough for her.

That night a friend whom Caroline often prayed with, Barbara, called her and told her that her husband couldn't join tomorrow's prayer meeting because of his work. The following morning Barbara came to Caroline's office and they talked for a while. With a bright smile on her face, Barbara suggested that they start the prayer time with 15 minutes of silence. But during this quiet time, Caroline couldn't concentrate; the strange client cancellations were still bothering her.

After the silence, Barbara shared how during the week prior her husband, Mark, had exploded with anger over his parents after they invited him to a conservative church where the pastor preached that nonbelievers would go to hell. Barbara said, "Mark was so hurt by this message that he left the church and he's questioning the Christian faith altogether. But when we have our open conversations here at our prayer meetings, he has always seemed to wish to want to live a life of faith." Now Barbara was anxious that her husband might turn away from that.

Then it was Caroline's turn to share what had happened during the week. She talked about her frustration with the clients canceling and her burning desire to find an answer.

Barbara soon took out a small note pad from her purse and put it on the round table in front of them. A verse from

Paul's letter to the Romans chapter 12 was written on it: "Do not be conformed to this world, but be transformed by the renewing of your minds, so that you may discern what is the will of God—what is good and acceptable and perfect." She then asked her friend whether she wanted to do a spiritual reading practice called Lectio Divina, or Divine reading, with this passage. Caroline agreed and hoped that she could get some spiritual insight into her concern.

During a Lectio Divina reading of a Biblical text, a passage is read three times. After the first reading, each person chooses a word from a passage and repeats it silently. After the second reading, each attends to the feeling or image that come up within them. Finally, after the third reading, each person listens to what is God like for him or her in that word or passage, and for what he or she might be called to do.

Barbara repeated the verse and the words, "Renewing of your mind" touched her heart. Caroline was inspired by, "Discern what is the will of God."

Then Caroline read aloud the text once more. This time when she meditated over the phrase, "Discern what is the will of God," she had a vision: Five or six small plants were placed in a circle around what could have been a space for writing. That space was now blocked off. But then a large hand appeared and rearranged the plants in a linear fashion. Now the space was accessible again and there was plenty of room for her to write.

After their third reading, Caroline felt she understood the vision for the most part: The plants seemed to represent the several kinds of work that she was engaged in such as seeing clients, group supervision, teaching, learning classical guitar, and writing. She had thought that all her work was important, but she realized that the moving of the plants seemed to be indicating a new priority. "Some things God may want me to do first, and others later," she said.

Eventually, Caroline rearranged her time so that she could begin to write her book. Writing filled what was missing in her heart with a renewed happiness. Her clients rarely canceled and even her busy workdays were filled with new joy.

Caroline's insight that day also spoke to Barbara and her concerns about her husband. Barbara felt that it was important at this time for her and him to focus on the open conversations at their prayer meetings, allowing much time to voice skepticism.

Spiritual Practice

(1) How have you experienced a nudging of the Holy Spirit that called for your attention?

(2) How did you respond?

(3) When you followed that spiritual nudging, how did it affect your life?

Prayer

Holy Spirit, help me tune into your wise direction so that I can prioritize my work.

(30)

In Great Despair

"O Lord, be gracious to us; we wait for you. Be our arm every morning, our salvation in the time of trouble."

—Isaiah 33:2

Timothy had the weekend off from his work. After he had a restful night, he awoke and was lying on his bed listening to the raindrops. He felt at peace and thought to himself how nice it was to rest at home on such a rainy day and spend time with his wife. He could hear Florence now in the kitchen calling him, "Tim, breakfast is ready. Wow, look at this heavy rain! I hope that my lettuce in the garden will be okay."

After some silence, Florence came to Timothy and told him that she had just received a text message from their good friend Melanie. She needed to take her husband, Kurt, to the psychiatric unit because he was threatening suicide. "She doesn't know what to do and wants to talk to you," Florence said with emotion.

Timothy called Melanie immediately and told her that it would be best to go to the emergency department at the nearby hospital and that they would meet her there. When they arrived at the hospital Melanie's younger brother was in the lobby and told them that Kurt was in a treatment room. Melanie came out and gave them an update, "Kurt talked with a doctor and they're now waiting for another psychiatrist. The hospital only allows one visitor at a time so if you guys can come back later today or tomorrow, that would be great. Thank you so much for coming!" Melanie hugged them both close while she cried softly and asked them both for their prayers.

Timothy and Florence returned home tired and emotionally drained. Timothy took a nap, but Florence couldn't rest; she remembered Melanie's request to pray for Kurt and their children.

The next day Florence received another text message from Melanie asking whether she or Timothy could be with Kurt while she took a short lunch break. Florence texted back, "I will be there soon."

She met Melanie and was allowed to enter the treatment area.

Kurt was in the hallway waiting to be transferred to the psychiatric unit. When Florence stood by him, he said, "I am very scared, but I finally slept a little bit last night with the help of medications."

Florence held Kurt's shaky hand and prayed in silence, "Jesus, please hold Kurt and give him your peace."

Kurt sat in a wheelchair with a small bag on his lap and a thin blanket covering his shoulders. Florence was struck with how fragile and vulnerable human beings really were. As they walked through the long and gloomy underground hallway to the psychiatric unit Florence noticed the naked electric pipes, electric circuits, and the coldness of the concrete walls and air. She felt as if the underground hallway was a metaphor for Kurt's condition, and for anyone experiencing depression and suicidal thoughts.

Florence slipped into her own reflections. It came to her that anyone could fall into such a depressed, confused and hopeless situation. "I receive so much strength and hope from my faith—I pray it will carry me when I have to endure such deep despair."

When they finally arrived at the psychiatric unit, a guard allowed only Kurt to enter. Florence remained alone in the hallway, waiting for Melanie. After she arrived, they talked for a while until a nurse called her into the unit.

Florence noticed it was getting dark outside, so she walked to the parking lot, feeling how very tired she was.

That night Florence couldn't sleep; tears rolled down her cheeks and she couldn't understand why. As she sobbed, she prayed, "God, we are so weak and fragile. Have mercy, Your mercy, on Melanie and Kurt."

At the end of the week, Timothy visited Kurt. Kurt was still in the psychiatric unit and a nurse explained to Timothy that Kurt was currently in treatment but that he might be discharged in the afternoon. Timothy then gave the nurse an envelope for Kurt. Inside was a prayer that Timothy had written for his friend:

God,
I am powerless over these terrible thoughts and
    sad feelings.
I need Your help.
I will not act on the terrible feelings,
I will not keep them,
I will let them go,
and I won't take them too personally.
Help me.

God,
I surrender.
Please penetrate these terrible thoughts
and sad feelings with Your Light,
for then they will not overcome Your Light nor
    mine.
And I trust that in this emotional chaos
there will be creativity and purposefulness
and that I don't need to know the answers today.

I would like to be a hand for Your peace
and I am open for Your peace.

Kurt was discharged that afternoon. He gradually became better with medication, therapy, his loving family
and friends, and moved into a clearer path forward.

Spiritual Practice

(1) What has helped you when you have gone through
emotional confusion and helplessness?

(2) If you pray, how has prayer helped you let go of negative emotions and thoughts?

(3) Might you have friends who could pray with you in times of distress?

Prayer

God, grant us a desire to learn to pray so that we can see the Light in times of hopelessness.

(31)

Sue and Robert Give and Receive

*"He [Jesus] put before them another parable:
The kingdom of heaven is like a mustard seed
that someone took and sowed in his field; it is the
smallest of all the seeds, but when it has grown it
is the greatest of shrubs and becomes a tree, so
that the birds of the air come and make nests in its
branches."*

—Matthew 13:31–32

Robert worked part-time at a non-profit organization promoting social justice.

One of Robert's colleagues asked him if he was interested in being a manager at a local Quaker Meeting House campus. Quakers called their churches Meetings because they believe that church is everywhere and not confined to a building. This particular Meeting House was a hundred years old and the property included three buildings in addition to the main house that were used by a preschool and an elementary school. There was also a separate building with an apartment in which Robert and his wife Sue would receive free rent in exchange of their duties.

Sue was enthusiastic about the idea. In her prayers, she asked God whether they should take on this position. The Meeting campus was very peaceful and the apartment open and inviting with a tall pine tree that provided shade.

As Sue was praying, she felt a deep peace and soon knew that this peace was God's guidance. Feeling a deep sense of peace was her way of discerning a Divine leading.

Two months later, the couple moved in with their new title as "Resident Friends." Quakers called themselves Friends, as Jesus did with his disciples.

Their new home and position kept them on the go; it seemed that there was always something that needed attending: phone calls, plumbing, broken air conditioners, creating a parking system. Robert developed a fee schedule for community groups for the use of the facilities. They managed the calendar and particularly enjoyed being able to offer space to those groups at a very low rate.

Because the campus was open and located on a busy street in the heart of an economically diverse area, homeless people would occasionally ring their doorbell and ask for money or food. Sometimes a homeless person would spend the night on the campus. Robert and Sue tried to find a balance between safety and allowing for a welcoming environment that also created a safe place for homeless to sleep.

The couple liked their work very much. Robert enjoyed seeing Alcoholic Anonymous (AA) groups gather in the Fellowship Hall of the Meeting House.

In time, their caring and open hearts attracted more and more people who wanted to use the Meeting House. Members of the Quaker Meeting were glad that the house allowed new service projects to grow and thrive.

One night, Sue returned from work just before 11 p.m. and parked her car in front of their apartment. Just as she was about to open the front door, she noticed what looked like a freshly polished ball lying next to the door.

When she bent towards it, it moved! The "polished ball" was in fact the bald head of a homeless man. He had found a place to hide and sleep behind the bush next to their front door and used the landing of the steps as a pillow. He pulled back his head in surprise and looked up at Sue.

"Madam, may I stay here one night?" Sue was a little surprised herself but pretended to be okay. Several homeless people had slept in the back of the building, but no one had yet to make their bed right in front of her apartment.

This man didn't look like many of the other homeless who often carried sleeping bags and other personal belongings with them. Instead, he wore a clean, white shirt and long pants and didn't appear to have a sleeping bag or anything else with him. Sue thought that this was strange, but she said to him, "Sure, you may sleep here tonight."

A short while later she saw Robert parking his car and walk toward the door of their house. Sure enough, a moment later she heard Robert's voice quite loud, "Oh, sir, you surprised me! What are you doing here?"

The man replied, "Sir, I am sorry. I just got out of prison and didn't have any place to go tonight. Can I sleep here just this one night?"

Robert said, "Yeah, you can sleep here. But you are wearing only a shirt and it is going to be cold tonight. Do you need a blanket?" The man responded, "Thank you, I am okay. I promise I will leave early in the morning."

Robert entered their apartment and asked Sue if she had seen the man next to the front door. "His head was so round and shiny under the moon that I thought it was a soccer ball," he exclaimed. "I almost kicked him!"

Sue smiled and replied, "Yes, I just had the same experience!"

The couple found a warm blanket and pillow and Robert handed it to the man. "Just leave it on the doormat tomorrow morning," he said, and the man thanked him kindly.

Robert sat down on the sofa with his wife. "What a place," he said with awe. "Many people rest in and around this church." They were both struck with the importance of their surroundings in the community and the role they played as facilitators.

For nine years the couple served many different people as caretakers of the Quaker Meeting campus. The memory of their independent yet likeminded response to this homeless man gave them much joy for years and strengthened their relationship. They continued to serve and to grow spiritually—just like that tall, strong, and sheltering pine tree.

Spiritual Practice

(1) Do you have a special, blessed place?

(2) When you are there, in what ways have you experienced blessings?

(3) How have you been a channel for blessing other people or a community in this space or in another capacity?

Prayer

God, thank You for Your blessings through caring for people and the community.

(32)

Salome Reopens Her Heart

"The earth is the Lord's and all that is in it, the world, and those who live in it."

—Psalm 24:1

Salome and her husband, Jonathan, liked sunflowers.

In spring their garden blossomed with particularly beautiful sunflowers, roses, and delicious raspberries. Their living room door faced their garden and Jonathan replaced it with a glass door so that they could view their flowers even from within their home. A particularly tall sunflower radiated its beauty in front of a small kumquat and a tangerine tree.

One day Salome found that the head of that big sunflower had fallen on the ground near the kumquat tree. She thought that the head was so heavy that the stem couldn't hold it any longer. Strangely enough, however, the stalk of the sunflower was indeed strong. She then noticed that half of the seeds of the larger yellow head were gone, and she wondered how they had simply disappeared. She gathered the remaining seeds and scattered some around the garden and some to share with her neighbors.

When she awoke the next morning, the seeds of her other sunflowers were gone as well. It was quite the mystery!

She went to take a closer look at the flowers and, sure enough, the heads of the smaller sunflowers were gone as well. Yellow sunflower petals were scattered all over the front yard. All seven sunflower stalks were now without heads.

She was beginning to get just a little angry.

"Perhaps it was the squirrels that ran around on the porch?" she thought to herself. She began to research ways to prevent further damage to the sunflowers and discovered one way was to sprinkle red hot peppers around the area.

Salome was reminded of a dream Jonathan had the night before of a thief jumping onto the table in their living room. She felt that the thief was real and actually in her garden.

The next few days she watched the behavior of the squirrels. A new, beautiful sunflower had just blossomed, and she sprayed it with the hot pepper.

A few days later, however, it rained. Jonathan looked outside and exclaimed, "Look, oh no!" They both watched as a squirrel had somehow reached the head of the sunflower and was now breaking it off right in front of their eyes. Salome groaned, "I think the rain washed away the sharp smell of the pepper!"

Salome watched with growing contempt as the squirrel nibbled away at the sunflower head. But then, suddenly, she looked at the small animal in a new light and began to feel sorry for it. She thought, "Maybe that squirrel was very hungry."

Several questions came to her mind: "Do I really own those sunflowers? I was not the one who planted them, after all. The birds were the ones who dropped the seeds so that Jonathan and I could enjoy their blossoms in our yard."

She then began to think about how recently in her medical office her number of patients had dropped. She had had some bad experiences with insurance companies that didn't pay so she started accepting only those that actually paid the claims.

It occurred to her, "Am I supposed to be the one to decide who can and cannot receive treatment in my office? Didn't I pray to God that this office be a place for everyone to come for rest and healing?"

She was surprised to notice how she had yielded her heart to insurance money without being aware of it. She was playing God on the throne deciding which patients should receive treatments and which should not. The money from the insurance companies had determined her choices.

Salome cried, "God, forgive me! Everyone can come to this office and get treatment regardless of what they can handle financially." She was filled with grace and found her heart opening once again.

A week later, her friends visited them from out-of-state. They brought a bunch of big sunflowers as a gift. Salome smiled when she received them.

The squirrels in her yard had brought her stolen heart back to her. She was reconciled that all things belong to God, the true Owner of creation.

Spiritual Practice

(1) Has your heart ever been closed to a particular situation?

(2) Where and in what way was your heart not aligned with your conscience and faith?

(3) What led your heart back to yourself or God?

Prayer

God, help us to guard our hearts with diligence so that they may not be stolen from us or compromised, and that they may be aligned with Yours.

(33)

Awakening

"Even though I walk through the darkest valley, I fear no evil; for you are with me."

—Psalm 23:4a,b

Michael was a 25-year-old student majoring in business administration. Having formerly worked in marketing, this subject was a logical step, but his heart was not in it.

Despite his many abilities, he had severely low self-esteem. When he was a teenager, he learned he had been conceived before his parents were married. This made him feel uncomfortable and insecure. "Was I really wanted?" he wondered. His mother had also told him she was very sorry that when he was a young child, she and his father had often left him alone.

At the university, he enjoyed living in a dormitory where he had made new friends and enjoyed communal meals and discussions on social and political issues with fellow students. And yet, despite his positive experiences, his low self-esteem caused him to occasionally feel rather depressed.

During the school term, Michael received a notice that his first-floor dormitory room was being remodeled into administrative office space. He was given the choice to move to another room either on the second or on the fourth floor. He thought about which floor to move to for several days but couldn't make up his mind. As time passed, the need to decide made him more and more confused.

This indecisiveness began to spread into other areas of his life, becoming worse as time went by. He would spend hours in the supermarket simply trying to decide which jam to buy. Eventually, Michael became severely depressed. Filled with self-hatred, he was most angry with himself for majoring in business administration and was certain that he was wasting the money his parents provided to support him.

Finally, Michael was admitted to the psychiatric unit of a hospital, but he continued to spiral downward; he stopped bathing, stayed in bed all day, didn't want to talk with anybody, and had suicidal thoughts. He was also so rebellious that he refused to take his medications and he yelled at the people around him.

His campus minister and his close friends visited him in the hospital and tried to console him. Before his hospitalization, Michael had appeared to be very self-reliant and independently following his unique path. It was hard for others to understand why and how he could suddenly become so confused, unable to make even the smallest decisions, and so dismissive of himself.

Michael felt as if he was walking in a deep, dark valley all alone, without any light or hope. He thought that this was hell.

While he was in his worst state and under 24-hour psychiatric observation, he received a letter that contained a prayer from his mother:

God, look at this young man.
You have burdened him
with an agitated mind.
He hates himself,
he punishes himself,
he overthinks his life.

God, I insist
that You do not want this.

I lay out this tragedy
in front of you
so that my son
will be filled
with the warm stream
of Your love.

I speak to You, oh God,
about this demon of hate
and destruction
so that You will defeat its power.

This I pray every day
so that my son will stay alive
and gain new life.

Let him be reborn
from the spirit of Love.

Amen

Michael read his mother's prayer and called the nurse. "Nurse, please read this, isn't it beautiful?" he asked her. Something in his mother's words touched him deeply and profoundly. Somehow her prayer had reached deep into his soul, and somehow, his behavior felt changed. The prayer had begun to set him on a path of healing, and he started to seek and accept guidance from the nurses and doctors at the hospital, and to show interest in the well-being of others.

The next day he was moved to an open unit since the staff trusted that he no longer required such close observation. He began working with a new psychiatrist and medication helped in supporting his newly found stability.

Later in the week, the new psychiatrist was able to reserve a hard-to-find spot in a rehabilitation center for Michael. When he arrived, he found the environment peaceful, very pleasant and supportive. He cherished the conversations with his therapists, and they enjoyed working with him. In art therapy, glimpses of hope began to shine in his paintings.

One day he tried horseback riding at a nearby stable and he was able to handle the horse very well. That surprised him and he felt good about himself for it, feeling a sense of self-esteem beginning to grow inside himself that he later shared with his therapist.

The dark lure of death gradually disappeared. He walked in the Light again. He thought to himself, "Heaven might be like this."

At the end of that year, on New Year's Eve, he quietly decided that he needed God to be able to live and he committed himself to an active relationship with God.

Spiritual Practice

(1) How have you experienced your own hell on earth?

(2) Did you somehow feel the presence of God even in those dark times?

(3) What helped you to return to the light and into a new and hopeful reality?

Prayer

God, be the center of my life. Help me to see the Light and have hope even in dark times.

(34)

A Five-Minute Prayer

"This is to me the hour of the greatest joy I ever had in this world. No ear can hear, no tongue can utter, and no heart can understand the sweet calm and the refreshing of the spirit of the Lord, which I now feel."

—Mary Dyer (1611–1660)

Kyle was a 60-year-old who had several successful businesses over the course of his life.

For several years, however, he had suffered from headaches that hit him hard intermittently. During his sleep, he tended to grind his teeth badly, which caused both the headaches and pain in his jaw. Several dentists had helped to ease some of the tension in his jaw, but the pain was still intense.

Kyle thought that grinding his teeth at night might be attributed to some psychological issue. He decided to visit Nora, a calm and spiritual counselor that he had met in his networking group.

Nora assessed his symptoms and asked when the grinding habit had begun, and he told her about a recent incident. As a business owner, he cared about the well-being of his fifty employees. One of them, Jim, was going through an exceedingly difficult time of grieving because his young son had died of leukemia. Kyle had raised funds to help Jim have enough money for his son's cancer treatment.

Despite all efforts, however, Jim's son had died. Kyle saw that Jim often shed tears in the middle of work. Jim said to him, "I miss my son so very much." It was not easy for Kyle to see Jim expressing such emotion although he knew how hard it was to deal with loss and had three sons of his own. The only thing Kyle could do was to give Jim big hugs.

He said to Nora, "It is so hard to deal with an emotional crisis such as what Jim is going through. It has influenced me a lot. I feel I am very lucky and I have no complaints. I have a good family and no financial concerns, and I am healthy except for the teeth grinding and headaches," he smiled, adding "You know that I am Italian—as long as I can enjoy meals with a glass of wine and friends, I am happy." He smiled.

He also told Nora that even though he had handed over his business to his sons, he was still the primary manager for the employees.

Nora listened to him for a while and then said, "Kyle, you seem to be carrying a big responsibility for your business and your family. I wonder how you have found peace to carry such a burden of caring for so many people.

Praying is one way to calm down. Do you ever have time to quiet your mind and practice prayer?"

Kyle looked at her and said, "I actually don't feel much stress because I enjoy my work and I like to bless other people. Before we start work, we hold hands and pray together. Only I seldom ask for anything for myself because I have received so many blessings, and I would feel guilty if I would ask for anything more. I'd rather pray for others."

Nora shared that she had read many articles on the effectiveness of prayer and that it was found to affect the part of the brain that holds emotions. She thought that a ten-minute daily prayer practice might calm Kyle's mind, ease his emotional tension, and thereby help relax his jaw muscles. Kyle agreed.

Nora suggested that they pray together for ten minutes now. Kyle agreed and prayed in silence, asking, "Lord, I need your peace." After the ten minutes had passed, he smiled. "Wow," he remarked, "this was not easy, but I really feel peaceful. I will try more often to pray for myself."

When Kyle returned home, he remembered that he had promised Nora to pray for ten minutes. It was too long a time for him, so he began to pray for five minutes every night before falling asleep. He would lie in bed and simply ask, "Jesus, help me not to grind my teeth."

He questioned if such a simple prayer could help him, but he enjoyed the peace he felt, nonetheless.

A few weeks later, Kyle met Nora in their business networking group. She smiled and asked him how his headache and teeth grinding had been. Kyle replied, "I know I promised you, but I couldn't pray for ten minutes every night. But I have managed to do five minutes most nights before I fall asleep, and it works. I don't have such intense pain anymore in the morning when I wake up. There is still some pain, but much less." Nora encouraged him to keep praying.

A year later Kyle took an important license examination for his business. It was a whole day of tests that covered various topics. The night before he was very anxious and couldn't fall asleep. He remembered the time he prayed with Nora and how peaceful he felt. He decided to pick up praying again that night. "Jesus, help me not to be so nervous and to feel your peace."

This time, however, he was disappointed with the result. He still felt the same nervousness and anxiety when he woke up the next morning. He knelt down and prayed, "Jesus, be with me today and hold me. I know with your help I will be fine."

Despite the pressure, Kyle felt a calm presence throughout the whole day of testing. He passed and received the new license.

When he met Nora again, she asked him whether he still enjoyed his five minutes of prayer. Kyle said, "I really appreciate that prayer time. I had let go of it for a while, but then I had to take a licensing exam, and I picked it up again. It worked to calm my nervousness and anxiety. I prayed for peace a couple of times even during the exam. That peace helped me to pass it and I got the license!"

Nora gave him a big smile and said, "Congratulations, Kyle. You have entered the world of prayer. It will bring you healing."

This time Kyle committed himself to continuing his daily 5-minute prayer practice. He still felt anxious from time to time, but he was grateful that he had found a way to find peace and remain calm. Occasionally, when he felt it appropriate, he told others about it.

Spiritual Practice

(1) Have you had a time when you felt frustrated and anxious despite all your efforts?

(2) What helped you to deal with the frustration and anxiety and refresh your energy?

(3) One resource may be a simple prayer. Write your own prayer—with your very own words—to feel peace of mind, console your soul, or give yourself courage.

Prayer

God, I ask You for Your peace and courage when I am anxious or frustrated.

(35)

Jeremy Finds the Love He Sought for So Long

"For God so loved the world that God gave God's only Son, so that everyone who believes in him may not perish but may have eternal life."

—John 3:16

Jeremy, a 52-year-old engineer, had been working for a telecommunications company for more than 20 years.

Since his divorce, his daughter, Annie, had gradually closed her heart to him. She was now in college and Jeremy wished very much to have a closer relationship with her. He missed her and often thought about the happy times he spent with her during her childhood. He often talked about his sadness, regrets, and longings with his older sister.

When his daughter was still a child, Annie attended a Bible school in a neighborhood church. Jeremy felt that this experience learning about the Bible together with other children influenced her very positively. So, after she left for college, he began to volunteer as a Sunday school teacher at the same church. He taught children about God's love and how it was expressed in Jesus Christ. By teaching the children in Bible school, Jeremy gradually came to understand his daughter as a child.

The Sunday school children raised some good questions: "Teacher, why do people say that Jesus died to forgive our sins? Why did he even have to die to show us his love for us?" Jeremy couldn't give them answers that came from the bottom of his heart. He only taught them standard answers that he was taught but he had never truly experienced love himself.

Their questions challenged Jeremy to reflect on his own relationship with God. His childhood had not been a happy one because his mother was often sick, and his father frequently traveled. His parents had not been accessible to him. Jeremy was always hungry for their love. He thought to himself, "No wonder I was so desperate to seek the love of a woman and marry early."

He remembered how happy he was when he and his former wife met. As time passed, though, their affection for each other withered. His life became centered on his work at a demanding job and his time off was spent investing in stocks to provide further financial stability for his young family. He had bought a family home and security, but he failed to notice how lonely and depressed his wife had become.

After the divorce, he lost hope. A major recession had taken away the financial stability he had achieved, and he felt a growing desperation; his wife was gone, his daughter emotionally disconnected, and he had barely enough money to get by. He was broke, lonely and nothing remained of his life as it had been.

Only his passion for finding love endured in his heart.

In his many moments alone, he thought about how much he related to the story in the musical "Phantom of the Opera." In the play, Erik, the ghost-like Phantom, had a secret love for the beautiful singer Christine. She, however, desired another man by the name of Raoul. Erik was born with a facial disfigurement and wore different masks as he sought Christine's love. Jeremy felt that he and Erik were kindred souls in some way, both seeking love that had always been denied to them.

In the musical, Erik eventually kidnaps Christine and brings her to his underground cave. He demands from her to decide between him and Raoul. He lifts his mask and wants to kiss Christine and although she is stunned by the scars on his face, she kisses him and he is overwhelmed by her compassion.

That scene touched Jeremy deeply. He, too, longed to be accepted with his wounds.

Jeremy gradually began to put his life back together. He enjoyed listening to Christian music and sermons at the end of his workday and in time he began to feel his scars and empty soul fill with new hope. One evening, one song particularly touched him with the lyric, "You are my beloved son." As he listened, he remembered the neglect and abandonment in his life. That night, a voice inside him said gently, "God loves you."

Jeremy realized that God had loved him all along and that God was hoping that Jeremy would love God back. He not only realized it, but he also felt it so deeply that he cried. As the tears ran down his face, he knelt before a small cross he kept. Jeremy felt as if his soul had finally found peace in the arms of Jesus.

Jeremy had finally found the love he had longed for all his life.

His caring for the children at Sunday school became deeper. He said to his older sister, "I will continue to pray and teach children that God loves everyone, even when we don't feel it, or don't think we are worthy, or can't even imagine it. Someday the one-sided love of God may turn into a mutual love as it was with me."

Jeremy continued to make efforts to reach his daughter Annie. Ever so slowly they were able to take small steps towards a loving and healthy relationship.

Spiritual Practice

(1) What have you been seeking throughout your life?

(2) Have you experienced broken or one-sided love?

(3) Where do you find the love that stills your deep longing?

Prayer

God, we long for love that soothes our soul. Help us draw that love from You.

(36)

An Amazing Team Spirit

"Two are better than one because they have a good reward for their toil. For if they fall, one will lift up the other."

—Ecclesiastes 4:9–10a

Sharon enjoyed the calm rooms of her office and the setting in the surrounding neighborhood. It was close to home so she could walk when she had time and prepare herself for work.

The office building was located on a cul-de-sac and when she opened her front door, she could enjoy fresh air, green trees, and views of nearby mountains. Most of the other tenants were pleasant and the rent was affordable as well.

For some time, however, she had noticed that clients from a rehabilitation center three units down were hanging out in the parking lot across from her suite, smoking and talking very loudly. The rehabilitation center helped people suffering from drug and alcohol addictions in their recovery.

The situation gradually became worse. Some of the clients stood facing Sharon's office directly, smoking pipes or vaping and creating clouds of disturbing smoke. People also drove into the parking lot playing loud music; the venue was quickly becoming more like a hang out. Sharon would go outside and politely ask them not to smoke in front of her office.

But the situation failed to improve, and in fact, began to deteriorate further. One time, she heard someone pounding on an outside wall of her office. Again, Sharon went outside and asked them to stop. Another time, when she opened her door for fresh air, a homeless man asked her for money while she was still with a client.

Sharon felt strange; it was very rare that she experienced such disturbances and solicitations at her office. But the bottom line was that she didn't feel safe anymore. She sent an email to the building manager about the crowds around her office and in the parking lot, but the manager didn't respond.

Soon other tenants complained about messy restrooms and the lack of security. A couple of Sharon's clients began to feel uncomfortable with the smoking and the people blocking the parking lot. Some clients canceled their appointments.

Sharon discussed the problems in her local business group. Their advice was simple and to the point: move out and find a new office.

But Sharon didn't want to give up and leave. Rents in other office buildings were expensive, and none of the locations featured such a nice entrance environment. She was actually glad that people with addictions were receiving help and felt that the community should support such efforts. If only the noise and the smoking would stop.

As time went by and the situation continued, Sharon became increasingly nervous and frustrated. She asked her prayer group to pray for her office situation.

One of her more charismatic-oriented prayer friends, Nan, visited her office and said, "Sharon, this is spiritual warfare." She went on to show her how to pray in order to cast out evil spirits. She asked Sharon to bring a bowl of water. Nan told Sharon to imagine a drop of Jesus' blood entering the water and spreading throughout the bowl. Then she poured the water with the imaginary blood of Jesus out over the parking lot. She prayed out loud, "I cast out the evil spirits here in the name of Jesus. This place be filled with the Holy Spirit!"

Sharon followed her and joined silently, "Lord, cleanse this area so that peace can return again."

The situation continued to exhaust Sharon. But she still didn't want to let go of her otherwise pleasant office; she struggled to find a solution.

One morning, the janitor visited Sharon and told her that someone had broken into the restroom the previous night and left a terrible mess. It meant a lot of work for the janitor. She said to Sharon, "There is this skinny, tattooed young man that comes here every morning. I am scared of him. He always walks around the parking lot with his dog, sniffing for something. I think he is looking for drugs." Sharon remembered that years ago, drug dealing was common in this area.

Later on, Sharon returned from her office dismayed and asked her husband, Luke, to pray with her. They were in the habit of placing their worries in God's hands. "God, what would you like us to do? Do we really need to move the office? Or is there some way for me to stay? Please give us wisdom to discern."

After they prayed, Luke suggested, "Why don't we visit that rehabilitation center and talk with them? Their clients seem to be the primary problem. Let's not accuse the staff there or blame them; let's just ask them to help us bring back the peace and quiet to our office building."

Luke contacted other tenants in the building before talking with the rehabilitation center and several of them joined Sharon and Luke on their visit. To their surprise, the staff told them about a recent break-in, and they apologized for their clients' inappropriate behavior in the parking lot in front of Sharon's office. They explained that the people smoking and making noise were not clients of the center but came to use the center's space for another organization's group meetings. Sharon and Luke were very glad that the people at the center were cooperative and supportive.

A few days later, Sharon found graffiti tags painted near her suite on one of the building's walls. Apparently, a gang was claiming her office building as its territory. Other tenants sent emails back and forth to one another and to the office manager, alarmed with the latest incident. At last, the manager made a belated apology and agreed to meet the tenants.

Luke called the graffiti removal department of the city and they responded promptly. Sharon felt things might finally be turning around and that the Holy Spirit was helping all the tenants to work together.

The staff at the rehabilitation center told Sharon that they decided to no longer allow groups not connected to the center to rent their rooms. They had also been trying to find a solution and just recently a nearby office space without neighbors had become available for these groups.

The change they had prayed for began in earnest: A new restroom lock was installed and soon after the noise and smoke disappeared.

Peace had returned to Sharon's office. The janitor visited Sharon and said with emotion, "I am so relieved! I was having trouble sleeping it was so bad. Your prayers really worked." She had tears in her eyes.

Sharon was overjoyed. Not only did the calm and quiet return, but the whole struggle had served to bring all the tenants closer together, including the rehabilitation center.

She said to her husband, "This is incredible! Your idea to talk with the center opened the door to work with other tenants. With everyone united together, and with the help of the Holy Spirit, we were able to stay."

Luke and Sharon laughed and gave each other high fives.

Spiritual Practice

(1) Have you faced a seemingly impossible-to-overcome situation?

(2) What was your approach to coping with that situation?

(3) Do you think it is possible to invite the Holy Spirit to work together with you and your concerns?

Prayer

Holy Spirit, I invite you. Come into my life and guide me in my current situation.

(37)

Emma Thinks About Everything Again

"For surely I know the plans I have for you, says the Lord, plans for your welfare and not for harm, to give you a future with hope."

—Jeremiah 29:11

Emma had owned and operated her own pharmacy for more than ten years. She was contracted with several doctors in the same medical building and enjoyed a robust business.

When a new medical group purchased the building, however, Emma could not keep ownership of her pharmacy. She had been working with one physician in particular who sent his patients to her, but he moved his office clear to the other end of town.

It was very sad for her to have to leave the business she had built and the environment she had cherished.

Emma called her older sister, Tina, and shared what she had been going through. She asked Tina to pray for a new job.

Emma's friend Marian was also a pharmacist. When she heard of Emma's situation, she hired her on part-time at her own, much larger, pharmacy.

Emma and Marian often talked together about their Christian life. Every day Emma read the Bible and it was a very important part of her life. They had known each other well over the years and Emma felt that Marian might be a good employer.

Despite her high hopes, Emma soon became disappointed by Marian's emotional ups and downs and her unpredictable behavior. Marian frequently reduced Emma's hours and changed her schedule arbitrarily without consulting her.

Emma was confused. She asked herself, "Is this the person I have known?" She began to get upset, especially because her income was not enough. To make matters worse, Emma then received a notice and was told to leave within two weeks. Marian had gone out of town and couldn't be reached.

Emma was now furious; she felt betrayed and couldn't sleep for several nights. She couldn't understand why Marian acted like that. She consulted with other friends who had worked for Marian, and it turned out that they had had similar experiences with her.

A few days after Emma was laid off, she woke up early and joined a prayer meeting at her church. When she opened her Bible, she noticed that the last date that she had written on one of the pages was in January, four months prior. Somehow, since she began working for Marian, she had stopped reading the Bible.

Emma's heart had lost its space for listening to the word of God. She hadn't prayed much anymore, either, and she wondered why she had stopped. Was it out of frustration over having to give up her own pharmacy? Was she just tired? She didn't know.

She thought to herself, "Neglecting my spiritual practice may have been one of the reasons why working with Marian didn't work out. I was not inspired by the word of God and was not coming from a place of peace."

Emma thought of the prophet Nehemiah in the Old Testament. He was sent to rebuild the walls of Jerusalem. But because his neighbors kept blocking him, he couldn't finish the work. Emma felt that just like the unfinished walls of Jerusalem, her relationship with God had been blocked. The break with Marian re-centered her on God.

Her anger toward Marian lessened.

The next Sunday in her church, the pastor preached about how Jesus was betrayed by some of his closest disciples. He said that many Christians take advantage of Jesus for their own benefit. Emma thought that her own experience of betrayal and hurt was actually rather small; she felt peace.

Another week later, Emma was invited to a dinner that honored people like herself who contributed time and funds for a program to reduce hunger among children in Africa. As she sat at the table together with other sponsors, she felt as if God consoled her with the warm recognition she received. God seemed to encourage her to keep doing her good work.

After the dinner, Emma called her sister, Tina, and told her about her experience of how God's word began to inspire her again. She was also happy that she was able to send toys to a missionary in Mongolia who worked with local children there.

While she was still on the phone with Tina, another call came in. She phoned her sister back a few minutes later, "Tina, I was just offered a job!"

Tina was excited for her sister, "That is great news! I hope it will work out better. Just don't let go of Marian completely. She made an effort to offer you a job when you were without any prospects and in a difficult place. Who knows what her situation is now? She might be going through troubles of her own. Keep her in your prayers and it may help both of you to heal. It might also be easier to pray for her now since you have some distance."

Emma reflected on all this again; her sister had a point: Emma had never taken the time to consider where Marian might be in the midst of the situation. Emma had been consumed by her anger and feeling of betrayal. She prayed, "Jesus, help me to pray for Marian so that I can see her efforts on my behalf. I pray that in the future she will find a more positive way to help others."

Emma's life became more open after this. She tried to appreciate the intentions of people, even if the outcomes were different from what she expected. She used her time to read the Bible and continued doing good work for others.

She thought to herself, "Marian's behavior felt very dismissive. It hurt and it is a big challenge to rise above disappointments and I can't always do it. But when I can, it just feels so good. It feels like I am really partnering with God."

Spiritual Practice

(1) When you were deeply hurt, what was your response to it?

(2) How did you deal with your sadness, anger, and frustration?

(3) Did anything block your healing?

(4) How do you want to welcome a new beginning?

Prayer

God, I ask for Your healing energy to flow into my deep wound. May You help me to express my anger and frustrations in a healthy way, and not to hurt myself or others.

(38)

The Dash Is What Matters

"You show me the path of life. In your presence there is fullness of joy; in your right hand are pleasures forevermore."

—Psalm 16:11

Joan and Mateo were very grateful for their neighbors. They helped to take care of their garden and the wild cats and birds there. When the couple would travel, the neighbors would also watch over their house.

Joan especially liked her neighbor Catherine who lived just next door. Catherine gave Joan a Taiwanese lettuce plant to make the empty front yard attractive. Sometimes Catherine brought homemade honey and fruits and Joan enjoyed learning more about gardening from her.

One evening the couple heard that Catherine's mother, Avis, had passed away the night before. They were invited to the memorial service the following Sunday afternoon.

Mateo sent a condolence card to Catherine and her 90-year-old father, Fred.

At the service, Joan spent some time reading the little hand-out about Avis' life. She saw her dates of birth and death, 1932–2013. As she looked at the years, Joan remembered one of her HIV-positive patients whom she worked with as a counselor. The patient had complained about his life for many years, until he spent some time employed as an aide during funeral services. He had told her, "Joan, my work at funeral services changed my perspective. I learned that what really matters in life is that dash between the year of birth and of death."

Joan was curious about Avis and her life. Only once had Joan spoken with Avis and it was very briefly when Avis and Fred had stopped by Joan's house. Avis was sitting in the passenger seat and said "Hello" to Joan; she had already become very weak and didn't speak much anymore.

At the memorial service, family members shared about Avis' life: She and her husband were married for 62 years, and she had worked as a secretary at a Lutheran church where she had met Fred. They bought a house around the corner from the church and had raised four children in that congregation. And now she would be buried there. Joan thought what a blessing it was to have such a spiritual community.

Avis and Fred had remained faithful to the church even as attendance dropped and the church struggled with keeping its property. When Avis' health began to deteriorate, Joan often saw Fred sweeping the church's front steps alone, even as he himself was getting weaker, his back crooked and his hands shaking.

Joan listened to the many memories being shared about Avis. The church was full of people, and she saw many familiar faces. Avis' four children sang a song and Catherine, wearing a red jacket, shared a lovely story about how her mother would encourage her to wear red. She said, "I wore the red jacket in my mother's honor today." The sharing was peaceful and touched with humor.

Avis, it turned out, was a woman with a big heart for everyone she encountered. She invited neighborhood children and youth to her backyard pool. She was an avid gardener, and when her flowers were in full bloom, she would encourage people to come and pick them.

For a while, Avis and her husband had rented an upstairs room to a seminary student from Africa. He also spoke at the memorial, "I rented a room from Avis and Fred on the second floor of their house. Avis invited me for dinner every Wednesday night. And when I had to travel, she stood at the corner of the street and watched me drive away until she could no longer see my car. I never received such kindness and attention," he said as his voice trembled.

Even when Alzheimer's disease forced Avis to move to a nearby nursing home, she continued to play the piano and asked anyone passing by to come and sing with her. She shared her kindness even as her health continued to fail her.

After the service, there was more time for fellowship and a large reception meal. People greeted one another and former members of the congregation who had not seen each other for a long time had tears in their eyes as they met. "How have you been?" and "We haven't seen each other for such a long time!" could be heard throughout the hall.

Joan thought that Avis had created such abundant life with her generosity, her love for people, her music, and her faith in God. If Joan hadn't come to Avis' memorial service, she would have remembered her only as a weak, old woman.

On her way home, Joan said to herself, "Yes, what really matters is the dash. Everyone is given a *dash* and living such a full life as Avis did is truly a Divine blessing."

Spiritual Practice

(1) What is a great gift that you want to cherish in your life?

(2) How have you celebrated that gift? With whom and in what way?

(3) How do you live more meaningfully and abundantly to allow yourself to become who you are?

Prayer

God, thank You for giving me the opportunity to live a life, *a dash*. Help me to live my unique life fully and as You intend it.

(39)

Grace Experiences How She Can Appreciate That of Others and Her Own

"The Lord bless you and keep you; the Lore make God's face shine upon you, and be gracious to you; the Lord lift up God's countenance upon you, and give you peace."

—Numbers 6:24–26

Rachel was a retired history professor. She was witty and humorous, and remained active in her Jewish synagogue. Rachel also enjoyed praying together with Christians and spending time with a Brethren Christian group. Once she told her Christian friend Grace, "I don't mind being evangelized," as they laughed together.

On the first day of the Jewish New Year, Rachel received a call from Grace asking if she could come and explain Rosh Hashanah (the Jewish New Year) and Yom Kippur (Day of Atonement) to her Christian prayer group.

Rachel was grateful and happy that Grace had asked her. The prayer meeting fell on the second day of Rosh Hashanah and Rachel explained to the group that Jewish New Year observances stretched over a ten-day period. During that time there are services in which the people pray for repentance while each individual examines their omissions and sins.

Yom Kippur is celebrated on the tenth day, on which the people fast and believe that God seals the book of life for the coming year.

Grace said that Rosh Hashanah and Yom Kippur reminded her of Lent (the "spring season") in the Christian tradition. Lent, too, she explained, is a time of renewing oneself through self-examination, fasting, and repentance, all in preparation for the Easter celebration.

When Rachel talked about the concept of God's forgiveness during Yom Kippur, it seemed to differ from the Christian understanding of God's forgiveness. Traditionally, Christian teaching had instructed that forgiveness came about through the death of Jesus on the cross.

According to Rachel's explanation, God in Judaism may or may not forgive each person's sins. Rachel said, "The central theme of Yom Kippur is the effort by people to correct their behaviors. Whether God forgives sins or not is up to God." This reminded Grace of other Christian understandings of the way forgiveness came about, through repentance for example and God's unconditional love.

Rachel then asked the group whether they could see other similarities and differences between the two holy seasons. Grace shared that Christians could appreciate the practice of Yom Kippur due to the common theme for self-reflection and repentance that existed in both Christianity and Judaism. She liked the idea of repentance in the Yom Kippur practice. At the same time, for Grace personally it was liberating to believe that Jesus forgave her sins once and for all by dying on the cross.

At the end of their prayer meeting, Pat, another participant, said to Rachel, "I would like to join in the fasting on Yom Kippur. That will help me as I reflect on my relationship with God and cleanse myself of wrongdoings." Rachel was very happy to hear that.

A few days later, Rachel received another call from Grace who told her that she had shared her joyful learning experience with her husband, Chris, especially the traditions about the last day, Yom Kippur.

Grace looked forward to her experience of fasting, out of her personal appreciation for what she believed that Jesus had done for her. Chris suggested inviting Rachel at the end of Yom Kippur for the fast-breaking meal.

Rachel gladly accepted and asked whether her son might join the dinner, since they wanted to attend a Yom Kippur service together prior.

As the sun set and Yom Kippur ended, Grace finished her work and walked to the Chinese restaurant where they had agreed to have dinner together. Rachel, her son, Ben, and Chris were already there and welcomed her. Ben was a very likable first-grade teacher. He enjoyed the open and unencumbered minds of his young students.

Ben was still single, which for a moment was part of the conversation during dinner. Grace said, "In my culture a son who is single and lives in the same city as his mother typically lives with her so that he can save up some money." Rachel said, "I did suggest that to him." Ben replied, "Does that son also enjoy an independent mind?" and they all laughed; Ben was as witty as his mother.

They ordered a dish with various kinds of fish and vegetables and a sizzling shrimp soup. Each spoke about their own experience of Yom Kippur and Rachel said that their books had been sealed for the coming year.

On their way home, Rachel and Ben shared their mutual good feelings about their fast-breaking dinner experience. Grace and her husband were also filled with lingering amiable thoughts. Grace remarked, "What a happy and meaningful New Year's dinner."

Spiritual Practice

(1) How do you prepare to welcome a new beginning? Do you have a ritual?

(2) If you have experienced participating in religious practices that were not in your tradition, did you notice similarities?

(3) In participating in other religious practices, what was encouraging? What was challenging?

Prayer

God, thank You for giving us time to reflect on ourselves and to appreciate our faith with other members of Your human family.

(40)

The Common Plot

"All go to one place; all are from the dust, and all turn to dust again."

—Ecclesiastes 3:20

Helen was a long-time member of a Quaker Meeting community who lived to be 85 years old.

When she passed on from this life, Olivia, a friend of Helen's, heard that there would be a burial service for her. Olivia wanted to say "good-bye" to her friend and invited her husband, Jeffrey, to accompany her to the service.

While they were driving to the memorial site, they talked about cremation and different burial ceremonies in the Christian tradition, and what they liked and didn't like. They didn't really know what they would want for themselves honestly, and they were curious about how Quakers buried friends in their religious community.

At the cemetery, Olivia's attention was caught by words written on the wall in one corner: "Common Plot." It marked the site where the ashes of Quakers who chose to have no marker or name were laid to rest. It was the common plot—everyone together.

It had rained in the morning, and it was still cloudy in the afternoon as Olivia and Jeffrey walked around the cemetery before the ceremony began. They returned to the site of the memorial and the area marking the common plot.

The person at the Quaker Meeting who had taken on the responsibility of arranging burials had prepared the site by digging out a two feet deep hole. He pulled out a bag from a small container in which Helen's ashes were kept. Olivia remembered words of God according to the Bible, "You are dust and will return to the dust." She was deeply moved.

The arranger of the burial, bending over to enlarge the hole, sang in a soft voice, "Nobody knows the troubles I've seen; nobody knows but Jesus."

Then the ceremony began. Twelve guests gathered to form a circle around the site and held a steady silence.

After some time, one by one, friends shared memories about Helen: She was a passionate activist for women's rights and had experienced a very tough childhood but had moved beyond it to help and influence many people's lives. One of Helen's friends recalled, "She helped so many. The way that she helped to improve the lives of the poor was amazing."

Olivia remembered that Helen had adopted a girl from China. Helen had loved classical music and her daughter had also shared that love and had become a professional violinist. Helen had also supported many music students at a local university. As a political science professor, she saw herself as a spokesperson for the poor and the powerless in Mexico and the United States. She never married.

Another friend of Helen's shared that she had a strong and vibrant life energy. At one point, she was able to fight back against an aggressive cancer and even her doctors were surprised that she had lived well past the timeframe they had estimated for her.

Olivia thought that Helen had fought a good fight and lived a meaningful life. She had overcome her own troubles and committed herself to social justice and to making the lives of others better.

When the sharing of memories had come to a close, the friend arranging the burial used a small hand shovel to take some of the ashes from the plastic bag and pour them into the prepared ground.

One by one every guest in the circle took the shovel and placed ashes from the bag into the ground. When it was Olivia's turn, she poured ashes and said very quietly, "Helen, I love you." The next person poured ashes and mixed in a little grass and green leaves. Jeffrey took his turn and placed a small shovelful with a solemn face.

Finally, it was time to fill the remaining space in the hole with dirt, and again everyone participated.

After the ceremony, some friends of Helen remained and talked more about her. It was a while before people left, seemingly hesitant to say their final goodbye.

Back in their car, Jeffrey said to Olivia, "What a beautiful and meaningful ceremony; it was so communal with everyone participating. What an experience it was to take that shovel, remove some of Helen's ashes and pour them into the sacred ground, and then to pass the shovel on to the next friend."

Olivia agreed, "Yes, I am glad that Helen was buried in that common plot, together with her friends who loved her and shared her life of faith."

Spiritual Practice

(1) When you think of death, what kind of images or words come to you?

(2) Have you thought about how you would like to be remembered and laid to rest?

(3) Have you had to say good-bye to a loved-one or a close friend, one who shared their life with you? If not, how would you like to say farewell?

Prayer

God, thank You for reminding us of the unique person that each of us is in the cycle of life. Help us to live a life with reverence to You and others.

(41)

Healing

"You who have made me see many troubles and calamities will revive me again; from the depths of the earth you will bring me up again. You will increase my honor, and comfort me once again."

—Psalm 71:20–21

Klaus was awaiting his approaching 50th birthday and he was excited. His father had planned to visit him and so did his younger brother Bernard. It was going to be a great time together, last not least because Klaus lived far away which made family visits always very special.

When he heard that his other brother, Philip, couldn't visit because of work, however, he was a little bit sad. His parents had divorced when he was 12 years old. His mother had visited him only a few months prior to his birthday and so when she called to ask if she could also join the birthday celebration, Klaus was a little hesitant to say "Yes," because his dad was rarely able to visit, and Klaus was very appreciative that his dad was able to come.

Klaus decided to check with his dad first to see if he would be okay if his mother would join the birthday as well. They decided that it would be very nice if his mother would join the weekend of the birthday and that the days prior and after Klaus and his father would still have enough time by themselves.

Klaus was in a prayerful mood. If his brother Philip would have been able to join as well, their original family unit would be together for the first time in over 30 years. It would have been a miracle.

He and his wife Chloe considered calling Philip to see if he could join after all, but they decided against it. They knew that Philip had surely been trying to find ways to join and they didn't want to pressure him and make him feel worse about not being able to come.

Klaus' father, Markus, arrived on a Thursday after-noon. They went for a short hike the first day and spent the morning of the second day fixing the canopy over Klaus' patio. They attended a small noon worship service. Next they had planned to stroll through the city but Markus told Klaus that he was rather tired and wanted to spend the afternoon at home for a nap and coffee.

Klaus was a bit surprised; his father was usually full of energy, and it was not like him to stay at home for a nap. Still, Klaus didn't make much of it and was happy to take a nap himself to be ready for the big weekend.

Klaus rested as his father sat in the living room by the window. Suddenly the doorbell rang. Klaus was expecting a package delivery and was glad it had arrived on time. But when he opened the door, there was no mailman and no package. He turned right to check the driveway: There was a person there covering their face with a newspaper!

"I came to deliver your hometown paper," said the mystery voice. It was Philip! Klaus shook his head, his mouth gaping wide. Whatever anxiety he might have had over the preparations for the birthday weekend vanished in a second. He was so happy, he could only stutter in awe and happiness.

Ahhh, so now he knew why his dad had wanted to spend the afternoon at home. Not only that, but he was told that his parents and brothers had planned Philip's surprise visit for the past six months!

That same evening Klaus' mother, Angelika, and youngest brother, Bernard, arrived. Klaus picked them up at the airport.

Everyone met in their small living room. Klaus was still completely astonished; their family had come together again as one. Despite the troubled times they had had, they were all well and in the best of spirits.

Delicious salad and soup, dessert, and wine warmed their hearts even more. They talked about how happy they were that they had been able to keep the visit a surprise. During the six months of planning, each had a moment when they almost spilled the beans. But their careful planning had worked!

Later at night, Klaus said to his wife, "I will never forget this wonderful love."

Saturday, Klaus' birthday (and that of his wife's as well) arrived and his special day began. To mark Klaus' milestone year, he and his wife had arranged to donate a public bench on a popular local hiking trail for everyone to enjoy. Klaus had sent a postcard invitation to a number of their friends to celebrate the installation of the bench. He and his brothers started to pack tables and chairs, plus some soup and bread for a little gathering after the dedication of the bench.

Around 25 guests, including the forest rangers, formed a circle around the bench and held a moment of silence. Klaus' father gave a short message in which he spoke of his hope that the bench would serve as a place for people to reconcile. Philip took pictures and Bernard warmed up the soup and sliced bread. It was a beautiful and sunny autumn day and Klaus enjoyed seeing his family mingle with his friends and guests.

He noticed that his parents were sitting on the newly installed bench and talking with each other. Klaus was happy that they got along so well. He thought to himself that the bench had already begun its service.

Later, his mother shared with him what she had said to his dad on the bench. She told her former husband that their divorce was not his fault alone and that she understood now that he had not been able to live with her. Though he was the initiator of great agony in their family, she had been feeling that she, too, might not have been able to stay in the marriage. She knew that her present partner was best for her.

She told Klaus that at that moment on the bench with her former husband, there was a sense of relief and forgiveness.

Sunday began with a hearty breakfast in their backyard. They laughed and talked over scrambled eggs and vegan ham. Philip took pictures of the beautiful orange tree abundant with fruit.

Later that morning they walked over to join worship at the local Quaker Meeting. For Klaus, it was a dream come true to sit in the pew with his brothers and parents in the church that had become the center of his spiritual life. During introductions after worship, he stood up and said to the congregation, "Today is a very big day in my life." One by one he introduced his family to them.

On Monday, his brother Bernard and Klaus' mother returned to their homes. Before they parted, Klaus' dad said to his former wife, "I appreciate what you shared with me, about our divorce, on the bench. It lessened the biggest burden of my life."

In the afternoon Klaus, Philip, and their dad went for a hike in the nearby mountains. Klaus listened to Philip's challenges with juvenile diabetes. Philip had never shared much about it and Klaus got to know his brother better.

For their final two days, they traveled to a Benedictine monastery that had become Klaus' and Chloe's other spiritual home. The abbot gave them a tour of the church and Klaus' father was very excited. He was a pastor and he said, "This is the first church that I have seen that has at its core, at its Holy of Holies, a Jewish ark of the covenant that contains the bread as the symbol for the body of Christ. This is a wonderful appreciation of our common roots."

The next day they headed to the nearby beach. Klaus taught his dad the proper movements of race walking. As he saw his dad speed down the beach, he reflected upon how healthy and alive he was, shouting, "Dad, keep up your good health!"

Then it was time for Klaus' dad and Philip to return home as well. Klaus waited at the airport and made a video of their plane taking off.

The awe of this special birthday remained with Klaus for a long time. His mother called him and said, "Klaus, our family gathering on your birthday was truly a miracle."

Spiritual Questions

(1) How have you experienced restoration from wounds in your life?

(2) What helped you in your recovery? A person, an occasion, an insight, or something else?

(3) What was healed in you? Perhaps others were healed as well?

Prayer

God, thank You for always helping us and offering ways to be healed, sometimes beyond our imagination.

Appendix

On Prayer and Discernment

Kwang-hee Park and Jochen Strack*

"Trust in the Lord, and do good; so you will in the land, and enjoy security.

Take delight the Lord, and God will give you the desires of your heart.

Commit your way to the Lord; trust in God, and God will act.

God will make your vindication shine like the light, and the justice of your cause like the noonday.

Be still before the Lord, and wait patiently for God."

—Psalm 37:3–7a

Prayer is a valuable resource when a person seeks wisdom for healing from within and from outside of him- or herself. It is a spiritual pathway to face wounds, create healing energy, and to grow an awareness that reaching deeper, farther and wider beyond ourselves.

---

*Jochen Strack received a Master's of Divinity and is a certified spiritual director.

Prayer means opening up to the spiritual dimension of one's personhood and then integrating it into one's life. The spiritual dimension influences all other dimensions of oneself: the physical, psychological, intellectual, familial, social, and societal. If the spiritual dimension is not well, the other dimensions are adversely affected.

Spirituality is therefore understood to be an internal part of every person. Its reality becomes most apparent when a person experiences or reflects about his or her soul, worthiness, meaning, purpose, and a deeper awareness of connection with themselves, others, and the Source. **Religion**, on the other hand, is a human construct. Religion is an organized method to connect to God, or the Source. Put differently, spirituality "just is," whereas religion is "a way to."

Along with the five senses of smell, taste, touch, sight, and hearing, there is also a spiritual sense. It cannot be measured. It does not follow logic. Nevertheless, an experience perceived with the spiritual sense is real and often profoundly meaningful.

Prayer, of course, can be practiced in many ways: Devotion, petitioning, thanking, crying out "why?"; and in listening, speech, song, even movement. In prayerful **discernment**, a person might simply lay out an issue in front of God and say, "Look, God, this is my situation." He or she then spends significant time listening to what comes up in response within themselves—attending to what bubbles up inside. This discernment process can lead to what is often named the small still voice within, or the voice of **God**, the Light, or Christ within. God truly knows and understands.

There will always be a level of uncertainty whether what comes up within is indeed from God, or perhaps from the listener him- or herself, or other influences. Therefore this way of prayerful discernment takes practice, just like learning to play a musical instrument, and it is important to recognize that a person may never know if that which they receive in response is indeed from God. To claim absolute certainty can lead down a dangerous path of deception. But with practice, one will be able to still the voices of the ego, of society, and other influences. With time, discernment will lead ever closer to the authentic small voice within that guides towards healing.

One's healing will also be influenced by the **image of God** one has adopted. A traditional image of a dominant and controlling God may be comforting to some, while causing others to dismiss, run away from, or avoid God altogether. Such an image of a controlling God comes from the traditional belief that God has power over every situation, with or without considering our individual situation. This belief can stand in the way of a healthy growth in faith. It can make a person afraid of being closer to God, especially in times of great distress. Such a belief gives to God all responsibility for everything bad that happens. The image of God as all-controlling may also deny one's responsibility in participating in the healing of oneself as well as towards a world in which all can live well.

The stories in this book serve to show a different, life-giving image of God, one in which God and the self, God and creation, are interdependent. It is an image of God that will bring joy in working with God, in co-creating a world for one and all to live in harmony, empowering one another and appreciating diversity. God is Love.

God is connected to each person not only from the outside, externally, but also lies within each person, internally. That is why every person can listen to that small still voice within, to the voice of God, the Light, the Christ within. As nurturer and source of life, God relates to us all in every moment. The more an individual tries to open to God's presence, the more she or he will experience God as a loving companion and healer.

When a person understands God and him- or herself to be interdependent, prayer becomes an important channel to communicate with God. Through prayer, one learns how to open to God as source of wisdom and healing. God's creative energy flows into all lives. Each person can flourish. In prayer we offer ourselves to be God's hands in creating a world where all can be well, all can flourish— ourselves, our friends and family, and even those who oppose us.

As a person seeks in prayer to follow God's suggestions, or the will of God, for oneself and the common good, it is only natural that anyone may fail in following God's suggestions. No one can know or understand every deep pain and struggle, every deep need in the world. It is then that prayer becomes an opening for the life and love of God to flow into a person, promoting well-being, even when the person doesn't know where and how. God knows and understands. God always suggests ways that nurture life. Prayer creates a mutually empowering space in which oneself, others, and the world collectively can grow.

If practiced regularly, perhaps even daily, prayer enables an individual to be free from the bondage that they may carry consciously or unconsciously. It develops the inner strength to face deep wounds. Once healing has occurred, over time, prayer becomes a channel to find one's calling in nurturing others. It leads to acting respectfully towards all creation. It offers meaning. The person may become aware of their connection with God and feel God's presence, even in seemingly insignificant moments.

Prayer may help in:

- Coming to a clearer and calmer mind, and receiving new perspective, such as for a specific situation or need.

- Promoting healing by discovering one's shadows and unshackling patterns of (self-)defeat, allowing the stream of healing energy—God's grace—to reach oneself and others.

- Becoming more aware of one's connectedness with one and all, and developing loving relationships with oneself, others, animals, nature, and God.

- Finding meaning by caring for issues beyond oneself.

- Living in awareness of the Divine will and increasing the capacity to discern good and evil.

Some of these aspects of prayer can be found in other modalities for healing, such as psychotherapy. Certainly, prayer cannot necessarily replace psychotherapy, but prayer has a unique ability to create a relationship with

God and foster the spiritual reality of oneself, which sustains and nurtures all other dimensions.

When one's wishes, upbringing, society, or other influences confuse thoughts and feelings during prayer, words of wisdom as expressed in Scripture can help to re-focus on discerning God's will or calling.

A simple and practical way for daily Scripture reading is a page-a-day perpetual calendar of Bible verses or a church lectionary. One may also explore various ways to listen to readings of Scripture, such as through the daily podcast *Pray-As-You-Go* offered by British Jesuits, or the app *NRSV Bible for Everyone* with the *New Revised Standard Version* translation of the Bible (NRSV).

When working with Scripture, it is helpful to consider the literary and historical context of a passage, especially when a text does not appear to portray God as Love. The *New Interpreter's Study Bible*, based on the translation of the NRSV, provides excellent commentary by theologians from various religious backgrounds. Understanding the context allows for a better, deeper appreciation of how the wisdom in and behind the texts of the Bible might speak today to one's personal situation and the greater world at large.

A Prayer to Promote Healing

An example of a prayer that very actively promotes healing is the Lord's Prayer. It is a great way to connect and work with God. Jesus taught the Lord's Prayer in his Sermon on the Mount (Matthew 6:6–13). It has very practical implications for daily life, especially when adopted for one's own situation.

To do that, it might be helpful to write down the Lord's Prayer and then look at it verse by verse. Who is "our Father in heaven" for you? If it is an obstacle for you to relate to God as "Father" choose a word that will nurture you, such as Mother, Light, or Love.

If God's "will be done *on earth as in heaven*," how might that inform a decision you are facing, in light of God's desire to nurture?

When the prayer asks, "Give us this day our daily bread," one person might think about a financial challenge while another might ask not to suffer from anxiety or depression today—only today, one day at a time. Yet another may have a different concern. This simple request may help the person to be less worried, strengthening him or her to be better equipped to live in the moment.

The Lord's Prayer moves on to address one of the great healings that a life of faith offers: forgiveness. The prayer is asking to truly forgive, "As we also have forgiven our debtors." The act of forgiving and asking for forgiveness is an act of spiritual cleansing. It means letting go of ill intentions and thoughts, self-defeating emotions, and destructive behaviors. Forgiveness heals wounds and moves towards the love of God.

Though what a challenge forgiving can be! But here the Lord's Prayer assures us that we are not alone as we summon God to, "Guide us in times of trial and rescue us from the evil one." (This is a common recent translation of, "Do not bring us to the time of trial.") In other words, "Be with me, God, I want to walk with you." In such times of trial, the prayer is prompting to actively connect with God, especially when a person may be tempted to let their ego or emotions take over, or when one forgets that God wants to help on a path towards wholeness, for each and all.

At times one might experience confusion in discerning the will of God even though a person is in prayer or reads Scripture. In these moments, it can be helpful to consider how God expresses God's will through others or particular circumstances. For example, a door to a new opportunity may open or it may close, or being able to observe others' choices in a given situation may reveal a new option that had not been considered. Or God may choose to give comfort and guidance through nature, such as a beautiful sunrise.

At other times, nothing at all may seem clear. A person may see no way forward or may not notice how God creates new beauty and harmony out of confusion, tragedy, or loss—things God never wills. Continuing a prayer practice becomes even more important during these times. An answer may not come today or next week, but practicing prayer can carry a person through in good times or bad times.

Everyone will experience highs and lows in practicing prayer. Yet daily practice, even as short as five minutes, though it may seem insignificant, will grow to become a foundation for healing and wholeness, gradually opening our spiritual eyes, and may enable us to become aware of the nurturing presence of God.

Each of us will live with the One who forever and always is, and who promises, "I am with you."

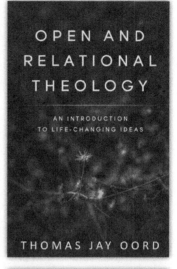

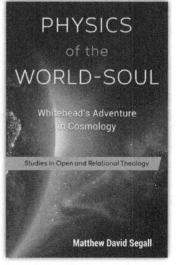

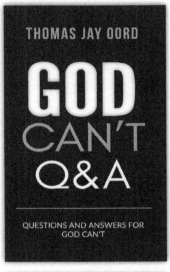
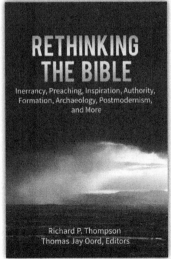
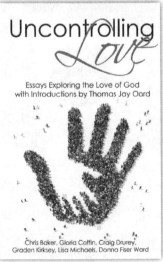

Made in the USA
Las Vegas, NV
01 October 2021

31473305R10132